From Where I Stand

From Where I Stand

Minority experiences of life in Britain

Edited by Desmond Mason
Drawings by John Gooch

Edward Arnold

© Edward Arnold 1986

First published in Great Britain 1986 by
Edward Arnold (Publishers) Ltd,
41 Bedford Square,
London WC1B 3DQ

Edward Arnold (Australia) Pty Ltd,
80 Waverley Road,
Caulfield East,
Victoria 3145,
Australia

British Library Cataloguing in Publication Data

From where I stand: minority experiences of
    life in Britain.
    1. Great Britain——Emigration and immigration
    2. Great Britain——Social life and customs——1945—
    I. Mason, Desmond
    941.085'8'0922   DA125.A1

    ISBN 0-7131-7489-7

Text set in 11/12 pt Paladium
by Colset Private Limited, Singapore
Printed and bound in Great Britain by
Richard Clay Ltd., Bungay, Suffolk

Every effort has been made to trace all the contributors, but the publishers will be pleased to make the necessary arrangement at the first opportunity with any author whom they have not previously been able to contact.

Contents

Acknowledgements

The publishers would like to thank the following for their permission to reproduce copyright photographs:

David Richardson pp 10, 66 & 110;
The High Commission of Trinidad and Tobago p 24;
Tony Smillie p 28;
National Library of Jamaica p 32;
London Express News & Feature Service/John Frost Historical
  Newspaper Service p 40;
Punch Publications Ltd p 44;
Barnabys Picture Library p 86;
Peter Handford p 100;
Popperfoto p 104.

Introduction

Desmond Mason

Desmond Mason is 37 and was born in Bristol. He has an MA in Modern English and American Literature from the University of Leicester and has taught in colleges in London, West Africa and the United States. He now lives and works in Cumbria.

Two books of his own material have been published by Edward Arnold: This city life *(1979) and* Rough edges *(1983). He conceived this current project on his return from America in 1982 and describes its purpose as 'an attempt to undermine racism by showing common humanity speaking out from behind the cultural barriers present in modern Britain'.*

Thousands of years ago in the days of pre-history the people who inhabited Britain erected the great stone circles of Stonehenge and Avebury. They were small, dark-haired, swarthy-skinned people, but we know very little about them, for they and their culture were submerged beneath a flood of fair-haired, blue-eyed immigrants from south-eastern Europe and central Asia. The first wave of these immigrants brought with them the secret of making bronze. The second wave brought iron into Great Britain. Thus for as far back as it is possible to go the history of the people living in these islands has been a history of immigrants adapting and modifying the culture that existed here before they came.

When the Romans came to Britain fifty-five years before the birth of Christ, they found a land divided between warring tribes that spoke different languages. In the four hundred years that followed, before the collapse of the Roman Empire, these Roman immigrants and their attendant merchants and mercenaries brought their knowledge to these islands. They brought over many different foods and spices and drinks; they brought over the forms of art and literature, the building and engineering that gave Britain its first taste of 'civilization'. The slave-based Roman Empire was then broken by the waves of Vandals, Goths and Huns that surged across the Rhine and the Danube to destroy the power of Rome. The Romans left behind them a common tongue — Latin, and a common religion — Christianity, both of which survived the hordes of Teutonic immigrants who swept into Britain with

1

their own languages and culture.

Angles, Saxons, Jutes, and Vikings all came to live and settle here, to mix and intermarry according to their own rules and customs. No doubt there was plenty of distrust, prejudice and bigotry among them, but they were eventually sufficiently united to fight together under the banner of a common king.

In 1066, King Harold of England was attacked almost simultaneously by the armies of the Norwegian Northmen under Harold Hadrada, and by the latinized Northmen under William, Duke of Normandy. The English forces beat off the Norwegian attack at the Battle of Stamford Bridge, but were themselves defeated by the Normans at Hastings. And so the Normans came to Britain. From the resulting combination of the French, Teutonic and Latin languages evolved the English tongue that flowered with the writing of Geoffrey Chaucer and William Shakespeare and the language that we speak today. The French gave to Britain a centralised administrative and financial structure and built most of the old castles that survive today.

And so the successive waves of immigrants continued. From Belgium and the lowlands came the weavers and cloth-makers whose industry and skill laid the foundations of the great wealth of East Anglia. (The name of this area indicates that it was populated by immigrants — the Eastern Angles.)

An Englishman sent over to Europe to promote trade in the Low Countries learned about printing, the revolutionary new way of producing books that had been invented in Germany. His name was William Caxton, and he returned to England in 1476 bringing with him a fugitive printer from Germany named Wynkyn de Worde. These two men, an English scholar and a German immigrant fleeing persecution, established between them the basis of printing in England, which placed knowledge within the reach of much of the population. The book ceased to be a precious handwritten manuscript restricted to a few scholars, and all sorts of books, especially the Bible, became available to ordinary people. One consequence of this spread of knowledge was the weakening in the influence of the Roman Catholic Church. This resulted in the establishment of a number of rebel or 'Protestant' Christian movements, including the Church of England, established by Henry VIII.

The religious persecution that occurred during this period led to further waves of immigrants fleeing to 'Protestant' Britain from Catholic Europe to escape persecution for their beliefs. People freed from ignorance demanded the right to think for themselves, and when this was denied them, they 'voted with their feet' and left their homes in search of a better life.

This same process has continued through the centuries as people from different countries have come to settle in Britain for all sorts of reasons, and in doing so have made their contribution to the life of the country. The legacies of our own days of Empire-building mean that we now have many British people of Asian and African origin who have come to live here to seek a better life for themselves and their families. The wars and political struggles that continue to disrupt life on our planet still bring to our shores those who are in search of peace and tolerance in which to live their lives and follow their ways. Then there are always the adventurers for whom the lure of life in a foreign land is a sufficient attraction in itself. Some will stay here all their lives, and their children will become 'part of the furniture' of Britain. Some of them will move on in search of something different or better. Some will return to the homes they left behind. All of them, whilst they are living here, are bringing their own contributions to the cultural life of the country and providing us with a chance to learn about the people who live outside these islands, thus learning more about ourselves, the human race.

It is with this in mind that I have compiled this anthology. Having lived abroad myself as an outsider in West Africa and North America, I have been on the receiving end of both hospitality and prejudice, kindness and cruelty, and I believe that the immigrant to Britain has much to say that is of value to us. As we eat our Chinese or Indian food, our spaghettis or our Macdonald's hamburgers, it seems only right to remark that without immigrants to Britain, and without the gifts that immigrants have brought us, Britain would indeed have an alien culture to the one we know today.

Many of the writers in this anthology refer to their experience of prejudice, but it is important to remember that prejudice is not restricted to people of one race, colour or creed. It is a common reaction between people of different cultures: prejudice exists between Africans and Indians, Swedes and Danes, just as it does between English and French. In the North of England, a southerner is regarded with suspicion as an 'off-comer' in the same way that the Hausa people of Northern Nigeria look upon the Ibo people of the South with some mistrust. It seems that 'tribal' prejudice against outsiders is almost part of human nature. Theories of racial supremacy are quite a different matter, however, where prejudice is taken to extremes and dressed up as scientific fact. The idea that one race is genetically superior to another is a comparatively recent phenomenon, largely restricted to the lunatic fringes of western societies, or to a lunatic society such as was Nazi Germany.

We have a word in English that describes a fear of foreigners: *xenophobia*. It is a combination of two ancient Greek words: *phobia* derives from a word meaning *fear*, and *xeno* from a word meaning *guest* or *stranger*. Xenophobia is an 'immigrant' word. Who then is the 'stranger'? Is it the West Indian? the Pakistani? the Irishman? the Jew? the German? the Norman? the Saxon? the Roman? the Aryan? Because if they are all strangers, then who are we?

The other side of the coin
Wynette Scott

Wynette Scott was born in Birmingham and went to school in the West Midlands. She gained her B.Ed. degree in English, Drama and Sociology at the University of London Institute of Education. She has worked as a teacher, a tea lady, a shop assistant, and a Gas Board complaints clerk among other occupations. She has travelled to her family's country, Jamaica, on two occasions. At present, she lives in London and works as a freelance writer in her spare time. Articles and fiction have been published by the ethnic press.

Normally, I'd have let it go. Another bus would soon arrive, and it would be half empty. But this was the day that Penelope got promoted. It should have been me. I'd trained her, for goodness sake.

Breaking the habits of a lifetime, and nearly my neck, I ran for it. No way was that bus leaving me behind. Swift satisfaction followed when the draw of its increasing speed sucked me on to the platform. My eyes skimmed the lower deck. Sardines packed in a thimble. Upstairs, a lone seat welcomed me. I crumbled into it.

Immediately behind, a skinhead talked not so much to, but rather at, a brown-haired woman.

'So this black geezer says, right, "Gimme the money and I will go home" — bloody cheek.'

Turning slightly, I identified the owner of the voice. He reminded me of a half-scalped porcupine. His pimples reddened, as he treated the new member of his audience to a hard glare.

'So I says, "You clean them toilets like what Mr 'arris told you. Them floors should be so clean, we could eat off 'em." '

'What did he say to that?' Brown-hair was quieter, sounded bored.

'He says, right, "Where I come from, we don't eat off floors" — bloody cheek. He was well out of order.'

I bit my lip. I would not get involved. I didn't need it. Not with my manager's weird reasoning so fresh in my memory. What had he said this morning?

'You must appreciate that it takes more than experience. Other things need to be taken into account.'

'Such as what?' I barely concealed my anger. The fool. He'd bleated on about how the staff might question my authority. I appreciated more than he realized. He would not rock the boat by appointing a black supervisor.

To be fair, my boss was a pleasant man. Some might call him a coward with the brainpower of a demented worm, but I will say that he was, nevertheless, pleasant.

I started to sigh, but my breath caught on nostalgic barbed wire. Brown-hair's voice was familiar. So was the porcupine's. It must have been sixteen or seventeen years ago but it all flooded back to me. Susie and Stevie — the terrible twins. Scenes flashed in my mind like those on a rewound video, replaying the past.

We were the first black family to move into the street. Or the area for that matter. Dad had saved for two years to bring Mum and us kids over from Jamaica. I was probably eight at the time. Same age as the twins who lived next door. We had strict instructions.

'Keep away from the garden fence. They don't want nothing to do with us.'

I neither knew the reasons for this, or cared very much, for Dad's ruling gave birth to an adventurous game.

When he was on the afternoon shift, and the twin's father at his office, we were conspirators. We'd play 'chase' on the way home from school. They could both run faster than I could, and I usually got caught. To relieve the boredom, Stevie sometimes let me win. Susie never did. There was another game called 'flipping pennies'. Susie worked out a formula whereby she could always predict on which side the coin would fall. It should have spoiled the fun, but it didn't.

'Heads I win, tails you lose,' her sing-song voice repeated. And many was the time I would call, sure that I could beat her. Definitely next time. Or the one after that.

We found a gap in the privet hedge that lined the garden fence perfect for secret rendezvous. Many bubblegum cards were swapped, and I got to learn about the Daleks. I'd never actually seen them, because we didn't have a television. But the twins did, bringing the wonderfully frightening creatures to life for me.

Stevie was a useful friend to have. An awful giant of a boy — he must have been at least four feet seven — called Crispian, had a favourite pastime: he would shout 'Blackie' at me in the playground. But never, ever when Stevie was with me.

Whenever our parents were around, we ignored each other, but an incident early one morning changed the peculiar routine. I was skipping. A quick glance over the fence noted the twins romping as their mother looked on. The sun beat down. I heard Stevie say that he was thirsty.

'All right darling, there's some Blackcurrant juice in the larder.'

Minutes later pandemonium ruled. Stevie ran into the garden clutching his stomach. His face was crimson. Susie began to cry, his mother shrieked. The noise scattered the birds nesting in the oak tree.

'What the — oh my God! Somebody do something, for God's sake do something.'

Poor Stevie. He'd swallowed some paraffin, carelessly stored in a lemonade bottle. I ran all the way to the doctor's house and practically dragged him back with me. Not many people had phones then.

Every cloud, they say . . . The two families sailed through what I later labelled the 'honeymoon period'. Our mothers would chat about prices and Green Shield stamps. Our fathers still didn't have much contact, because Dad always seemed to be on shift work. As for me, I achieved a long-awaited ambition — playing in next door's garden. It was just like at the park, where the grass was a velvet blanket. They had a lawn-mower, just like the park keeper.

At close quarters, Stevie's mother reminded me of the lady in the washing-up-liquid advertisement. Oh yes, there was television too. I spent cosy evenings catching up on all that I had missed.

We no longer had to hide the fact that we were friendly at school.

Teachers were always comparing the twins. 'Stevie is such a friendly little puppy,' they would say, 'but so easily led.' His sister was, 'much too serious for a young gel.' I knew what they meant.

Her reserved nature made me uneasy. It wasn't until a particular art lesson that I understood why. Our teacher, Miss Sydney — a frus-trated sergeant-major if ever one existed — asked us to paint a self-portrait.

We couldn't be trusted with the powdered paint.

'I will not remind you of the mess made last time, or the fact that I had to clean it up myself. Today, I will give out one colour at a time. Monitors,' she paused, 'step forward.'

Susie scraped her chair away from our group of desks, reaching for the paint palette.

'Line up!'

A heaped spoonful of salmon pink paint was meagrely doled out to each monitor.

'Each monitor will take a little water to mix the paint —' she broke off irritably, 'What are you doing Stephen? I did not tell you to start. Put down your brush at once!' He shrank into his chair.

'When I give the word,' her radar vision failed to detect any further movement, '*then* you may begin.' Miss Sydney breathed in deeply, suddenly expelling the air.

'Monitors — mix!' In each group, the honoured pupils dutifully obeyed.

'Now then. Fold your ams so that you can listen with your fullest attention. Hands up if you have a square face.' Momentary confusion. Were we allowed to unfold our arms? And so it went on. When all our faces had been categorized into squares, ovals and many more, the ultimate order was given to paint.

Susie raised her hand.

'Please Miss, Lorna can't.'

'But I've told her to. Why not?'

'Because she hasn't got a pink face, Miss.'

I had come to this conclusion ten minutes earlier, but had not wanted to upset my teacher's carefully laid plans. The smell of disinfectant ever present on Miss Sydney's clothing swamped me as she strode to my desk.

'I'll have to go the cupboard. Really, this is most inconvenient.' Her dead-fish eyes fixed on my offending presence.

She took ages to find some brown paint. In the end, we had no time to paint anything. I got the blame, but I blamed the person whose mission in life was to remind me and everybody else that I was different. Susie. There were the endless questions.

'Why aren't the palms of your hands brown as well? Can I touch your hair?'

I preferred Stevie any day.

Suddenly, the honeymoon was over. Dad refused to discuss the whys and wherefores, but one thing was certain. The fence was once again out of bounds.

Looking back, I think I can pinpoint the change. Just before Christmas, another black family moved into the street. I called for the twins on Boxing Day, eager to see their toy-shop bedroom. The back door being open, I wandered into the kitchen. Their mother had her back to me, doing the dishes.

'Excuse me.' The poor woman nearly jumped clean out of her skin.

'Susan and Stephen are busy. And don't you ever come into my house as if you own the place again. It is *not* your property.' And then, almost to herself, 'yet.'

School was never the same again. Stevie became distant. But not Susie, worst luck. She continued to bombard me with a bottomless well of stupid questions.

The final nail in the coffin came a few weeks later. I noticed it immediately. A new, more solid back door had been fitted to the twin's kitchen. The old one leaned drunkenly towards our side of the fence, covering the gap. Shortly afterwards, the house went up for sale.

I'd often wondered what became of the family. Bitter regret was hard to swallow. It might have been better not to find out. Ever.

The lurching motion of the bus, inching through the traffic, brought me back to the present.

A hand pressured my shoulder.

'It is Lorna isn't it? Stephen, you remember Lorna don't you?'

Stevie no longer existed. Stephen gave me a look as alien as those Daleks we once enjoyed. He knew me all right. I could tell.

'I'm getting off. Quicker to walk. Late as it is.' He loped down the gangway, slowed down by his miniature-tank type boots.

We smoothed things over with an exchange of pleasantries and further exclamations of surprise.

'Stephen's got problems, by the way. He was unemployed for ages — hates the job he's in now.'

Well, he wasn't the only one.

'How about you?' Those searching eyes were at it again.

I was going to say that I was doing great, but then my annoyance resurfaced. I didn't pull any punches. Why should I? Susie didn't murmur the expected sympathetic noises.

'What are you going to do about it?' So matter-of-fact.

I respected that. I respected her. She had never made things easy for me, and I still didn't like her. But I knew exactly where I stood. I looked at this chic young woman, trying to see a little girl in a frilly dress — hair caught up with tartan ribbons. All I saw was the calm expression, accurately predicting on which side the coin would fall, even while it span in the air.

'What are you doing now?' I was curious.

'Studying law.' It figured.

The traffic was moving. In a rush, we said our goodbyes. In their own way, the twins were two sides of the same coin.

'Heads I win, tails you lose.' Maybe. But I'll tell you something. I'm going to trap the other side of that coin. The winning side.

I stepped off the bus, the musical taunt dying away down the tunnel of time.

Questions

1 What concrete examples of prejudice are shown in this story?
2 Given the fact that Stevie used to be friends with the narrator, what factors are indicated to account for him growing up into a racist?
3 The narrator seems to respect Susie right up to the end of the story. Why do you think this is so?
4 Do you find anything in the attitude of the narrator to admire or condemn? Give reasons for your opinion.

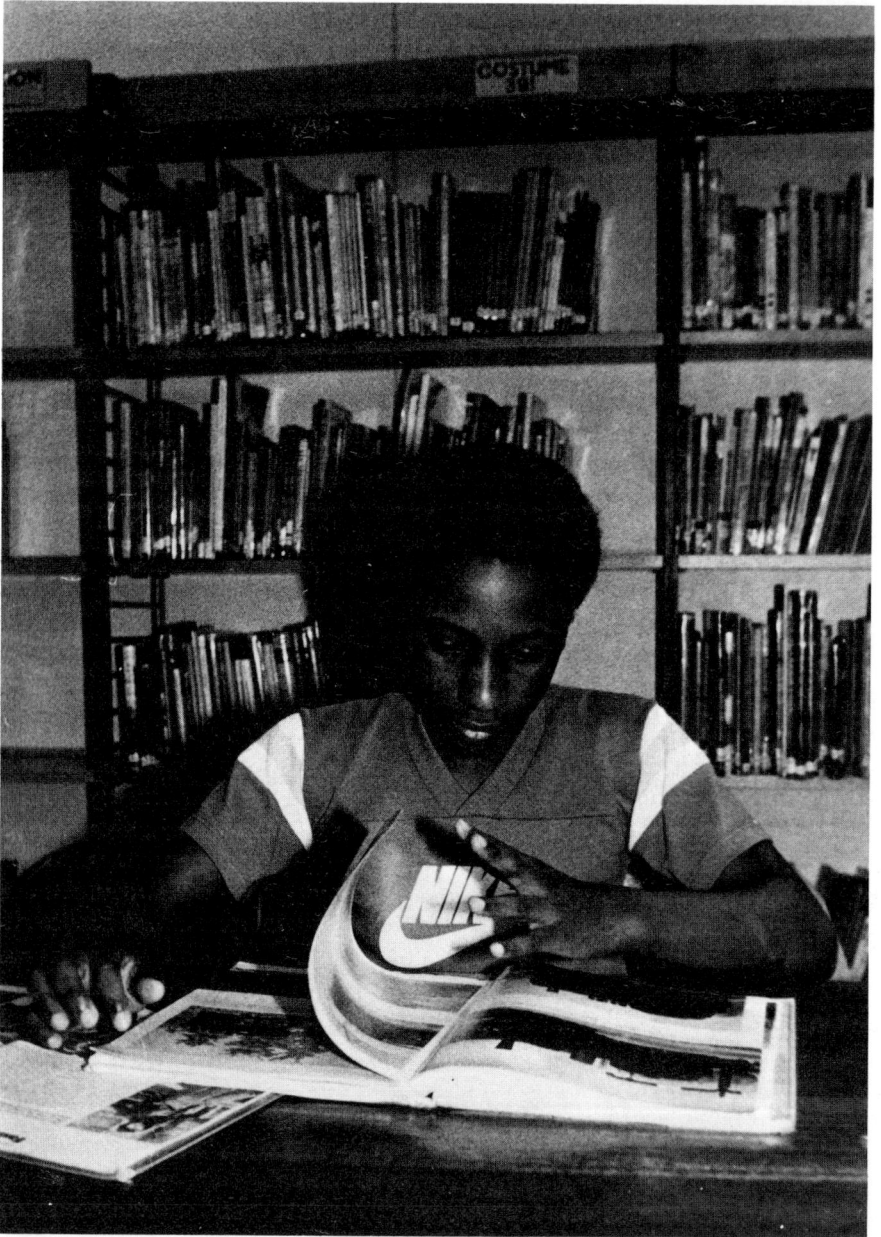

Coming from Dominica

Derek St Louis

Derek St Louis is 30 years old and came to Britain from Dominica at the age of 11. He has just completed a B.Ed. at Avery Hill College, London, having previously worked as a personnel interviewer, a sales clerk, a messenger and a youth worker. He has a keen interest in amateur dramatics and was once a singer with the cadence band Que Pasa.

We stood looking nervously at the door. The two Jamaican women who looked after the smaller children fussed around straightening ties and tightening hair ribbons. We had arrived at Southampton Docks from Dominica, and my brother Glyn, I, and about fifty other children were waiting for our parents. We, like most of the others, didn't know our parents, having been left in the care of relatives while they blazed the trail for us in the 'Mother Country.'

'Auntie', for that is what we called our great aunt, had been the one to coax and scold us through our early childhood. I remembered the way she had called out to me, 'David Baptiste!' as I was on the point of stepping into the boat and I'd turned and contemplated flying back up the jetty steps and into her open arms. Something, I'll never know what, had held me back. I'd stepped into the boat and been rowed out to the ship whilst exchanging insults with the Cork Street Gang who'd come to say goodbye to us.

Now, holding on to our suitcases with our names and addresses painted neatly on the side, we waited for our English parents to arrive. They came in dribs and drabs looking unsure. Some called out names and waited for shy responses, others simply scrutinized faces before bundling their long lost issue into unfamiliar winter wrappings. We watched, trying to match parents to children and hoping that no one unacceptable would claim us. In fact no one came to claim us at all that night. When everyone else had packed into the boat-train and gone, Glyn and I, Sweetman and Calvin were left behind, dejected. The Jamaican women tried to reassure us by saying that the ship would telegram our families. But that didn't make us less worried. Calvin started crying.

We stayed awake most of the night talking about what might happen to us. I hoped that we might be sent home but Sweetman reminded me of

11

the women's promise to cable our families. Glyn speculated on the possibility of getting a taxi to London; I reminded him that he hadn't the faintest idea where 84 Menton Road was, but he continued thinking up ways of getting us there by ourselves.

The next day the Italian nurse who had been in charge of us older children took us into the dining room and sat us among the upturned chairs while she tried to arrange breakfast for us. The waiter we had nicknamed 'Soup' came and chased us out. The nurse, after arguing with him briefly, led us away to the playroom and disappeared. I thought she looked as though she was about to cry. About an hour later she returned and took us to a part of the ship we'd never been to. We went up a short flight of stairs and into a room with thick carpets on the floor and chandeliers glittering above our heads. Some men in smart uniforms sat eating at a table. The nurse asked us to go and stand by the table. As we started towards the table an important looking man with lots of gold braid on his uniform got up and said something to the nurse in Italian and we were again ushered out. Some minutes later the steward we called 'Rapper' because of his habit of rapping people about the head, arrived at our cabin door with a tray of sandwiches and hot milk.

After the meal we wandered up to the deck through the eerie silence of the all but deserted ship. There was a pile of potatoes on deck and we amused ourselves by throwing them over the side until we tired of that and went back to the cabin.

Daddy arrived around four o'clock that afternoon. He put his head around the door and said, 'Hello'.

I knew it was him immediately because he looked just like Glyn. We shook hands, said goodbye to Sweet and Calvin, and followed him out, struggling with our luggage.

As we walked to the station through the streets of Southampton, Glyn expressed surprise at how warm it was and Daddy explained that the country was experiencing what they called an Indian summer. I wondered what it would be like when it got cold.

When the train arrived we sat in a compartment with two young white women. I studied them for a while but they seemed no different to those whites I had known back in Dominica. So I looked out of the window at the streets and houses that sped by. I remember being disappointed by how dull everything seemed and by the fact that I hadn't yet seen any skyscrapers. I'm not sure at which point my having stayed up half the night before took its toll, but when I woke up we were pulling into Waterloo Station. Night had fallen and there was a light mist in the air which I thought was steam generated by the trains. Everyone around us seemed in a great hurry to get somewhere. I wondered if they were rushing home to watch television. Daddy told us to hurry up and we followed him, still staring around us. Outside the station we queued for a taxi then drove off through the streets of London. Suddenly, for some reason I could never explain, I began to laugh. Daddy looked quizzically at me and asked what was funny. I couldn't answer anymore than I could stop laughing.

The taxi came to a halt outside a three storey house. While Daddy paid the driver I started gleefully up the front steps only to be halted by his voice, 'Where are you going boy? Downstairs we living'.

Slightly deflated I turned and followed him downstairs to the basement. There was a tall girl holding the door open and two faces peered from behind the curtains in the front window. The tall girl smiled and said hello as we went past. Beyond her Therese stood smiling, her hands on her hips. Therese, who at fifteen was two years older than Glyn and four years older than I, had preceded our arrival in Britain by two months. She'd been sent by plane because Auntie thought it unwise to send an adolescent girl on the cheaper but longer boat journey. It was the first time we three had ever been parted and I'd missed her terribly. Therese and I proceeded to hug each other while the others laughed. In the front room Glyn and I were surrounded by an assorted bunch of people.

There were two girls on the sofa, one about nine the other a few years younger, in addition to the tall girl who had now come into the room carrying a baby. Therese did the introductions. The tall girl was, as expected, Veronica. But she looked quite different to the first communion photograph Auntie had of her. The nine year old was called Cathy and the younger one Lucille. The baby was called Gary. I was surprised to hear that he was my brother because we hadn't been told about him despite the fact that he was almost two years old. A woman came into the room wearing a housecoat and slippers; she had cropped hair like a boy and was quite large. She threw her arms around us and kissed each of us in turn. I asked whether she was the cook. She looked as though she'd just been slapped and I suddenly realised my error. She was my mother. Wishing the ground would open up and swallow me I apologised, but Mammie didn't look mollified. I wanted to explain but couldn't.

The plain fact was that I had never seen a picture of my mother or father and often wondered what they looked like. To make matters worse, whenever we did something to annoy Auntie she always told us about our mother who wore stockings and high heels and walked through England's streets chip chip chipping like a lady while she had the worry of raising us. Thus for years my mental picture of my mother was of a lady in high heels, not a woman in a housecoat. Only servants like Beatrice wore bedclothes when they weren't ill. To ease the embarrassment Daddy suggested that we open the suitcases and give out the presents we had brought. Obligingly we produced the cacao, cannelle, guava cheese and the other things. We gave Daddy the bottle of Martini that we had managed to avoid the customs men taking, but they got the bottle of rum that Auntie had sent him and he would have to pay dearly to get it back.

That night Veronica sent Cathy to the fish and chip shop and I went with her. We walked along in silence for a while then I began to pump Cathy for information, 'What does Veronica do?', 'Where does Daddy work?' etc etc. She in turn asked all kinds of questions about Dominica and snakes and creepy-crawlies.

By the time I got to the shop I knew more about the family than I ever had. I'd also decided that I liked her. We had to cross the road several times on the way to and from the stop and I quickly found that though I wasn't particularly intimidated by the volume of traffic, I did resent having to wait so long to cross the street. However, since my tendency to race across had almost got me killed several times in sedate Roseau, I decided to bide my time and wait for the green man to come on as instructed.

Mammie had prepared a meal of rice and sardines when we returned from the chip shop and Glyn and I tucked in with gusto. Veronica offered us some chips but I didn't like the mushiness once you got past the crisp exterior so I rushed to the bin to spit it out. Everyone except Cathy laughed. She just looked at me as though I was mad. Then Glyn complained that he was tired, so Mammie busied herself putting down some old clothes to make a bed on the floor. Before we went to sleep we washed, using a plastic basin in the kitchen sink.

Next day at breakfast I amused everyone by declining a helping of 'big' beans instead of baked beans but nothing else happened to embarrass me. Veronica decided that she would take us on a tour of the house and introduce us to the other tenants.

The two rooms directly above us were occupied by a Miss Alva and a man known as Leftie. She was a light complexioned Jamaican woman in her late thirties and she had a kindly high pitched voice. She greeted our arrival with an excited, 'Is dem dis? What a way dem favour de Daddy'. Leftie was almost the exact opposite to her, being both squat where she was tall and slim and dark skinned where she was fair. Their voices too were comically dissimilar, his sounding like a barrel being rolled along the ground. Veronica said that he was an amateur boxer and that was why he was called Leftie. Glyn was quite impressed but I just wondered why he didn't have a broken nose like Celius back home. On the floor above them lived a Mrs Cunningham with her five children who kept up a barrage of noise as she tried to say hello to us. Eventually she gave up and went back into her room shouting. There were two other tenants in the house, but we were pointedly not introduced to them, instead we merely had their rooms pointed out to us. One of them was a young white woman called Sheila whom Veronica claimed was a trollop. The other was a Nigerian called Adeboye who was supposed to be mad. We met the supposed madman coming up the stairs as we were on our way down to the basement. Veronica whispered, 'It's him', and we fell into a self-conscious silence. He stared at us, his big eyes widening to give him the pop-eyed look of a frog. We hurried past him still in silence. As we rounded the bend of the stairs I looked back up at him. He was watching us from the landing, a puzzled look on his face.

Back in the safety of our basement I asked why, if he was mad, he hadn't been taken to the madhouse. Daddy, overhearing this, laughed and said that there was nothing wrong with him. Later on he played me some high life records that Mr Adeboye had loaned him. They sounded very much like calypso and made me think about Dominica, which made me sad. It also made me remember the day almost the entire ship's nursery had broken down in tears because one of the boys from Curaco had suddenly started crying about never seeing his grandparents again and started everybody off.

That evening we were sent to mass dressed in clothes we had brought with us. I was wearing my fourteen dollars a yard first communion suit and my clip-on bow tie. On the way to church I saw several people staring at me but I couldn't see anything wrong so I put their curiosity down to admiration for the cut of my suit. At the end of the service we stood around outside the church scrutinizing our fellow worshippers. I was rather shocked by the casual way some people dressed for church and voiced my opinion. Clearly embarrassed by this, Therese dragged me away muttering 'Render thy hearts' or some such thing.

Back home again we were sent out to play still dressed in our Sunday best. Our neighbours, the Flahertys, were in their garden. Cathy, who seemed to relish playing hostess, introduced us to Patrick and Sean who corresponded roughly to Glyn and I in age. They seemed nice and we started trading the sort of conversation about football and cricket that young boys inevitably do. Until, that is, Sean made some crack about the fact that I was wearing short trousers and wanted to know if we couldn't afford to finish the suit. Glyn, uncharacteristically coming to my defence, told Sean to, 'Shet up your mout!' and I, angered by the suggestion that we were poor, told him that he looked like a hungry lizard. We were warning each other of the dire consequences of ever daring to step over the wall into each other's territory when Mammie put her head out of the kitchen window and shouted at us to come in immediately. Meekly, we did as we were told, the Flahertys grinning triumphantly from their back step. Still angry about my clothes being laughed at I asked Veronica what was funny about them and she explained that English boys did not wear suits with short trousers and would think they were funny.

Slightly embarrassed by this revelation I went off to watch television. I was fascinated by the 'telly' because Dominica hadn't really entered the television age yet. Astaphan's, which was the largest department store in Roseau, had a large one on display, which relayed shots of the people shopping for the amusement of passers-by. In the evenings they switched it over the CBC company which relayed programmes from Barbados. Once I had got myself the beating of my life by going with Glyn to see a Lone Ranger film and staying out until eleven o'clock at night. Already frightened by my own affrontery at staying out that late, I was even more frightened by Primus who met me at the corner of the street to warn me that Auntie was going to give me a hiding that I wouldn't forget easily. Glyn, who was a renegade who frequently slept out, took his leave.

Abandoned to my fate I eventually plucked up enough courage to go in and accept the beating I knew was waiting for me. That night Auntie laid about me with a tamarind switch and made me go to bed without any supper, but I didn't feel particularly aggrieved. I knew too many parents whose punishment would have surpassed hers to feel misused. However, safe from censure in England, I settled down to becoming to TV addict. I got hooked on everything from 'Twizzle' to 'Peyton Place' and I often stayed up till both stations closed down for the night.

While I was busy getting TV eyes, Mammie busied herself trying to get us into a Catholic school. Daddy, who espoused anti-clerical sentiments, busied himself going to the pub after work in the evenings. Eventually a school was found some six miles away. For the interview we went dressed in the Dominican suits that we both now found rather embarrassing.

The school was like a glass palace, being mostly made up of huge panes of glass. The headmaster, who spoke as though he had hot potato in his mouth, wore a black gown like Quelch of Greyfriars and seemed oddly out of place in his glass palace. He invited us into his office and quizzed us about our education up to that point. Then he asked us what we considered to be easy questions about finding the area and perimeter of things. Finally, putting on his glasses and assuming his severest expression, he looked at Mammie and said, 'You are of course married?'

Glyn and I both whirled round to look at her. I'd never wondered whether my parents were married because in Dominica it simply didn't matter whether they were or not. Now it mattered a great deal.

Mammie was not amused by the question or the tone of the headmaster and snapped, 'Of course I am!' She fumbled in her handbag and produced the certificate. I wondered what the fate of most people in our house would be if they tried to get their children into St Ignatius' RC School.

A week later, decked out in our brand new school uniforms, we joined the Flaherty boys (with whom we had resumed friendly relations) at the bus stop and set off for school. Being first and second year students, we went to the annexe, which was a pre-war brick building with an interior of shiny brown tiles and polished wood floors. Assembly had started when we arrived, so we waited outside the head's office. Mr Barnett, the head of the annexe, was a gruff character with a pronounced London accent. He welcomed us to the school and sent us off to our classes accompanied by two boys he'd appointed as our guides until we got used to the system.

My mentor was a fair haired boy called Tony. He seemed genuinely pleased to have been chosen to ease my way into the school and between the office and our classroom he managed to convey that it was all right as a school and that Miss Tushingham, our class teacher, was nice.

When we arrived at the classroom I stood outside, unable to enter. Through the glass in the door I could see the assembled pupils. None of them seemed to be taking much notice of the teacher: the girls were chatting in a group at the back of the class; one boy was chasing another around the room, encouraged by the other boys; yet another boy was flicking pellets around the room with the aid of a rubber band. Tony's voice penetrated my consciousness, 'It's all right, come in'.

I followed him blindly; Miss Tushingham looked round and smiled a welcome. My entrance had the effect that the teacher had obviously been striving for and everyone fell silent. Miss Tushingham, a young woman with blonde hair and glasses, introduced herself and asked me to tell the class my name. My voice was so shakey that I had to repeat it twice and then spell B A P T I S T E so that she could write it down. Then, having got the attention of her students, she asked them to sit down before placing me beside a fat boy with red hair called Kiernan. Tony started to tell her that Mr Barnett had asked him to look after me but she waved him back to his seat and started passing some books out. When all the books had been given out she announced, 'We're going to do some reading aloud today'. There was an audible groan which she ignored. 'David, since you're new you can begin, turn to page twenty-five and read until I ask you to stop'. I could feel the class holding its breath as I began reading, but since English had always been my best subject and I'd practically lived in the children's section of the Roseau Library, I didn't have any problems with the reading, in great contrast with some of my new classmates who stumbled along as though they'd just learnt to read. When the fat boy beside me started to read he pronounced yellow as 'yellar'. I corrected him and was rewarded with a glare and the repetition of 'yellar'. I was scandalized that in England people spoke such bad English when I'd often been beaten for using local English and was totally forbidden to speak Creole.

When the bell went for recess the others all made a bolt for the door leaving me wondering what to do. A few seconds later Tony came back and said, 'Come on, it's breaktime, we can have a game of football'.

I couldn't think of anything I wanted to do less, since I was the worst football player imaginable, but I followed him out. In the boy's playground, where there were seemingly a hundred different football games all going on at the same time, Tony suggested that we got some milk before we started. I followed wondering what he could mean. Beside the gym a few crates of milk stood piled against the wall. He grabbed a couple and handed one to me. I looked at him dumbly. The idea of drinking cold milk horrified me. Back home no one ever drank milk without boiling it first. In fact we ate precious few things without cooking them in some way. Unaware of my revulsion Tony, who by now was on his second bottle, urged me to drink up. I put the bottle to my lips and sipped. The smell nauseated me. I felt certain that I would throw up if the milk reached my stomach.

Tony noticing my reticence said, 'You don't have to have it mate', in a voice that suggested exasperation.

I put the open bottle back in the crate and spat out. Feeling rather foolish I followed Tony back into the mêlée where I immediately collided with what looked to me like a full grown man in brown boots and jeans, who was in full pursuit of a ball. The man growled something about 'effing wog' and elbowed me out of the way. More shaken by his words than his action I walked away trying to think of an adequate reply.

Tony, possibly embarrassed by his failure to take care of me, said, 'Don't take any notice of him. He thinks he's a hard nut'.

I asked what such a big man was doing in the playground and he explained that my antagonist was one of the 4 L group who were leaving at Easter to find work. Obviously anxious for a game before the bell went, he then tagged himself to a group of boys playing one of the numerous games in progress, while I, declining his invitation to join them, wandered across the ground looking for somewhere to stand.

I was finally approached by a short Indian-looking boy who introduced himself as Da Silva and invited me to join a group of boys clustered around a hot air vent that blew warm air into the playground. The other members of the group introduced themselves using their surnames as Da Silva had done. They were Curry, Gould and Brown. I asked why they used their surnames and Brown shrugged and said that boys were always known by their surnames at school. Before we could get into any real conversation the bell went and we had to line up to go back into school.

At lunchtime Glyn and I joined up, more because he had the money than because we genuinely sought each other's company, since I unfailingly irritated him. Carrying our trays full of shepherd's pie and other delicacies, we found ourselves a couple of seats on a table with vacant spaces and sat down to eat. Here in the canteen it was possible to see the whole school for the first time. I observed that apart from Da Silva and a half-caste boy, we were the only black pupils in the school. We were aware that our arrival at our table had precipitated a sudden silence. We now became aware that everyone around us was staring at us as though we were spacemen. I felt a flash of heat shoot up my spine and set my ears on fire; my head also began to itch. I was acutely embarrassed. Glyn too seemed rather put out but, not knowing what else to do, picked up his knife and fork and started eating. I followed suit. The din resumed. Still racking my brains as to why they were so attentive, it came to me that they'd been waiting to see if we were going to eat with our hands. The realization stunned me. I felt my ears go hot again and struggled with an impulse to run out of the canteen. I opted instead to stay and play with the food which had lost all appeal for me.

I can't now remember most of that afternoon. I know that it seemed to drag interminably until at a quarter to four when the signal to rush home came. Mammie was going to work as I came in. She asked if I'd had a good day. I nodded yes and went to watch Twizzle and Footso.

Despite the horrors of the first day, I soon grew accustomed to St Ignatius'. What I couldn't get used to were the continuous slights and insults levelled against black people in Britain. The hostility was seldom overt, it came instead in subtle refusal on the part of shopkeepers to touch your hand when taking your money; in the refusal of young girls to sit beside you on the bus unless ordered to do so by the conductor. Then there were the people who stepped on your feet, pretended they had noticed nothing, and continued on their way. Others left train doors open if they got out before you, giving you the choice of being blown away or shutting the door. And there were always the 'no coloureds' signs in the windows of houses with rooms to let. Finally there were the whole catalogue of things you got called and the stupid jokes you had recounted about 'nig nogs'. For a long time I remained distressed by people who abused me because of my skin. But in talking to my family and other people it soon became clear that the only response was to fight back. The philosophy was never let someone step on your toe without stepping on theirs in return. We kept our resolve strong by continually telling stories of our encounters with hostile white people. When these rap sessions began they could go on for hours. Miss Alva, who was a profoundly Christian woman, told us that she had once been summoned for assault, after she had become incensed by the sight of a white woman spitting on a black child who had innocently asked her some question. Her pastor had gone to court as a character witness and she had got away with a fine of ten pounds, which she was well pleased with. Apart from this funny story, the one which amused us most of all was one related by a large Guyanese woman called Georgette who told us how she had coped with being ignored in a sweetshop while white people who had come in after her were served. She had waited until the shop had emptied of the other customers, and then spent fifteen minutes selecting sweets from the top shelf. Then she waited until the shopkeeper had weighed and wrapped them and then walked out, telling him what he could do with his sweets.

As well as unfriendly natives we also had to cope with what we considered to be a hostile climate. One evening as we were sitting curled in front of the telly, Daddy came in and announced that the white man we had been longing to see was outside. Rather puzzled by this, we went to the window to find that everything was covered by a thin layer of snow. Bursting with excitement we raced out to play in it. This was fine while we were running about in it but when we got back inside and the blood in our hands and feet began to warm up it was like having molten lead injected into the blood stream. I began to have doubts about liking the snow. As if to punish me for my fickleness in wishing its presence and then wishing it away the moment it arrived, the snow kept falling through the night. By morning the whispy layer had changed to a thick blanket which slowed everything and everyone to a crawl. The early snowfall was an omen of sorts, because it turned out to be one of the worst winters of the decade. Every day I struggled to school through what soon became slush and then ice. I always arrived at school chilled to the bone because it was a long walk from the bus stop and when I got there my problems still weren't over. Mr Hughes, my maths teacher, was an extremely sarcastic young man who took every chance to show up our inadequacies in maths by asking us questions we couldn't answer and then making smart remarks in front of our classmates. Since I was undoubtedly the worst at maths in 1A, Mr Hughes and I were soon at war. Having rather less in the way of arms I usually came off worse in our clashes. But my problems with Hughes soon guaranteed that a subject I had merely disliked I eventually loathed with every ounce of my being. Concerned to avoid one of our 'sparring sessions' one day, I sat in a geography lesson ignoring Miss Walsh and willing myself to be ill so that I could be excused maths. I succeeded after a while in making myself feel sick. By the time I got to the school secretary, I had broken out into a cold sweat and was feeling faint. The headmaster sat me down on a chair in the empty playground and administered smelling salts. I recovered just in time for the start of playtime.

Da Silva, Gould, and Brown, who had now become firm friends, congratulated me on my ruse but refused to believe that I had genuinely experienced the pains and nausea. Apart from hating all forms of figure work I also had one major problem with school and that was my failure to regulate my life by the clock on the school wall. I was always late. Glyn and Therese claimed that I operated on BMT (black man time) rather than on GMT which everyone else operated on (everyone else but me and low class black people).

BMT did not impress the staff at St Ignatius' and after putting me on detention several times, they began sending letters to my parents and Mammie started to nag me about getting to school on time. Around then my eldest brother Pascal came out of borstal. When he'd been sent there Mammie had written to Auntie saying that he had joined the RAF and Auntie who was intensely pro-British had been very moved by the news. The sordid reality had almost made me angry enough to write and tell Auntie the truth. Pascal was the apple of Mammie's eye and no one could say anything against him. He was continually asking her for money and he treated us younger ones as though he was our sovereign lord. One morning at Mammie's insistence he tried to hurry me off to school. I ignored him and continued getting ready at my own pace. Suddenly I felt a stinging blow at the back of my head. I turned round and shouted, 'Get off you bastard!' and continued at my slow pace. He hit me again and I started crying but didn't increase speed significantly.

He started shouting, 'Go to school!'; I held my ground and shouted defiance at him while he continued to rain blows on me. From the next room I could hear Mammie saying, 'Yes, make him go to school'. When Pascal grew tired of hitting me and disappeared into the toilet saying,

'You too damn rude' I picked up my satchel and left for school. I knew then that I hated them both and wanted to go home, back to Dominica, but I knew that the chances of that were small.

I took to spending any time in public libraries when not at school. I'd always been keen on books but now this love blossomed into a positive mania; I joined all four libraries between home and school and often didn't come home until they closed. I even walked around the playground with my head buried in a book. When I wasn't reading I was singing. As a small boy I'd spent hours pretending to be a carnival band leader leading an imaginary troupe of revellers and singing every calypso I knew over and over again. Now I wandered around pretending to be Stevie Wonder, Smokey Robinson and anyone else who was popular. One day I was prancing across the yard singing 'Signed Sealed Delivered'. As I got to the part that said, 'I'm yours', I opened my arms in a gesture of acceptance and a football hit me full in the face! Da Silva, who'd seen this, made sure that everyone heard about it and soon they started calling me 'Signsealed'. I didn't mind as it was infinitely better than the 'Blossom' they'd nicknamed me before, using the brand name of the boot polish to give me a doubly infuriating 'handle', it being both an insulting reference to my colour and a girl's name.

As time went by things started to improve at school. I excelled in all subjects save maths and games where I was, to put it mildly, appalling. My renown for being useless at those things spread so far that I stopped being embarrassed by it and started revelling in it instead. Glyn, who was always the direct opposite of me, was very good at both things and not very good at anything else. The fact that he was also lighter skinned than I often prompted people to ask if we had different parents. It was beginning to occur to me that English people really thought we were all what they habitually called us, 'black bastards'.

One day in Social Studies someone asked what the date was. Never one to simply say the number of the day, I recited, 'Fourth of October' and stopped dead. It was a year ago to the day that I'd arrived in Britain.

Questions

1 What particular aspects of David Baptiste's experience surprise you?
2 What does he find strange about Britain?
3 What sort of problems does David meet at school?
4 Describe the personal qualities shown by David in coming to terms with his new life.
5 What differences does the story suggest between life in Dominica and life in Britain?
6 In what ways do David Baptiste's problems differ from those of any native British boy of his age?
7 Write a paragraph describing what you have learned about Derek St Louis from reading his story.

Another life
Frederick D'Aguiar

Fred D'Aguiar was born in London in 1960 of Guyanese parents, but was brought up in Guyana. After completing his secondary education in London, he trained as a psychiatric nurse, then read English at the University of Kent. In 1983 he won the Minority Rights Group Award, and in 1984 the University of Kent's T S Eliot Prize. His first collection of poems Mama Dot *published by Chatto & Windus, won a 1985 GLC Malcolm X Prize.*

Remembered in flashbacks, particular flavours
Or smells, someone's gait or way of crossing
The room. It is brash and suddenly I am there
In a hammock slung between pines or a clean dive
Made into the shell pond, clear to the sandy bed.

This life hardly ever remembers it: streets surrendered
to traffic and police; and as if weathers for losing
tempers in or throwing up one's hands to outdoors
For months on end weren't enough — the unwelcome look
Or abuse: being told by perfect bare-faced strangers

'Fuck off nigger', before or after the pummelling,
Hateful, pathetic fits. Nursing these hurts,
There is only another life for comfort: the time
My uncle stepped on an alligator bridged across a ditch,
It scampered after him, we pained with laughter.

A new map of the world
Frederick D'Aguiar

1 The Cartographer's Nightmare

Who would have thought geography —
Its diamond certainty tread by us,
Could have come to this: politics,

The very contours, land mass,
Resources, disfigured like some
Wacky diamond formula deliberately

Wrong? Yet here's the map before me
With our original continent central,
Helplessly monumental, as never before.

Its regions etched and grained as if
You could trace the molecular route
Round its diamonds, mountains and sunsets:

Empire's down the drain, there's no
Imitating it; for once you've seen
A diamond-truth, where's the replacement?

2 Tradition

Here are the refined contours.
Revealed with another certainty —
A generations-old presence:

Childhood journeys through the curriculum;
A life-long climb up prestige ladders;
Street-clashes with those that harbour

Ignorant notions of our inferiority,
Whether in uniform or jackboots.
Having to burn angry statements

Into this Northern landscape, we've come to love
Like home; our youth burned and buried
In it; until it's a mother that can't help

Carrying us, feeding these sorrows;
And our joys — how we like to beat pan
And dance in the streets we wouldn't

Think twice about marching in.
Though the boundary's clearer nowadays,
There'll never be absolute peace between us . . .

The map shows burials, christenings,
Taut as a drum, its all puckered
With our protest, polished with our song.

3 Black-British

It's an island all the same.
The climate's harsher, surrounded
By a dull, oil-slicked, sea.

So we dream of The Islands,
As others dream, where the sun
Is the sole season ripening our ideals

Here our chlorinated thirst is unquenchable.
We grow-up with tar and cholesterol
And the same likelihood of an early

Cancerous death. And it's our metaphor
Of the decay from within as much as
Anybody's; still we dream of sunny

Islands where our world
Is a cast net, its leaden fringe
Formed in a perfect circle above shoals . . .

You can't map culture or desire —
Take a 'posse' following the same trend
Or 'Yow!' a call familiar as those Islands.

Questions

Another Life
1 What are the contrasts between the author's life remembered and his life in this country?
2 What are the most unpleasant of his thoughts about 'this life'?
3 What is the poem trying to describe?

A New Map of the World
1 In what ways does this poem differ from the first?
2 What similarities does it share with 'Another Life'?
3 What aspects of life here does the writer dislike?
4 Are the islands that the writer is dreaming of real islands? What do they represent?

Being black
Theresa McLean

*My name is Theresa McLean. I was born in Kingston, Jamaica, in July 1951.
I came to England in 1963 aged 12. I attended Baptist Mills Secondary
Modern until the age of 15 when I left to work in a clothing factory. At the
age of 19 I left to have my first child, and two years later I had my second
child. I did not work for the next nine years because I was busy bringing up
my children. In 1981 I did a TOPS course in a commercial college and at the
end of the course I was offered a job as an instructor, which I accepted. I
remained in that post until March 1985. At present I am employed as a temp.*

I have often felt the desire to put pen to paper to describe what it feels like
to be a black person in a predominantly white country. To describe how
it feels to have children hurl abusive and offensive names at you in the
streets, while their mothers look on approvingly; to be called names such
as 'nigger', 'wog', 'coon', 'sambo', 'nig nog', 'spade' and many other
derogatory terms so that it becomes a fact of life.

Different people react differently to this type of abuse: some respond
with verbal abuse, some with physcial abuse and some try to ignore it. I
personally fall into the latter category. This wasn't always easy to do;
many times my instincts told me to lash out blindly but I never did
because I knew this wouldn't achieve anything. Black people are always
accused of having a chip on their shoulders. This is true to a certain
extent. It is a sort of self-protection, a sort of armour against the prejudice
many of them have to face in their daily lives. I myself experienced things
like going into a shop and having the shopkeeper totally ignore my
presence, while they served people who came into the shop after me; or
going to the Post Office to cash my giro or family allowance, and hearing
somebody behind me refer to niggers who come to this country to
scrounge, or niggers who have colour TVs and drive big cars while they
are on the dole. It is hard to describe the emotions I experience at these
times: emotions ranging from intense hate to cold indifference. I have
often gone home after meeting this type of prejudice feeling very
depressed and defeated and feeling frightened. At these times I usually
feel the need to see another black face, to talk to someone who has been
there themselves, who has experienced this type of thing.

This is one of the main reasons why many black people like to live near one another, they feel safer in numbers. I have been living in England for eighteen years and for the first ten to twelve years I hardly encountered any prejudice at all, but for the past five to six years it has become steadily worse. I feel this has a lot to do with the emergence of neo-nazi groups like the National Front, the British Movement and many more like these. Experiencing prejudice on a regular basis can have a demoralising effect on one. You get to the stage where you are expecting to be insulted, expecting to be rebuffed and you have your guard up all the time. You begin to wonder if people say certain things to you because you're black; you ask yourself if they would have said the same thing to a white person; you feel yourself becoming paranoid.

Many times while walking along the street with my children I have seen groups of teenagers standing some distance ahead of us and as we move nearer towards them my little boy grips my hand tighter and tighter and he doesn't let go until we are some way ahead of them. He doesn't have to tell me that he is afraid at these times, I can feel it and I can see it in his eyes. He is used to gangs of boys and girls shouting abusive names at us as we go past. I often wonder what kind of effect this will have on him, if any, when he gets older. At the moment he is like any other happy ten year old, he seems to forget the bad things quite easily.

I don't want to create the impression that I am insulted by every white person I meet, far from it. I have met a lot of genuine people who really care about people, who treat me as an individual: as a person with a brain, with sensitivity and not some kind of imbecile who is unable to think or feel anything. There are a lot of white people who give up their spare time to go into immigrant areas to do community work, people who take the time to try and teach Indian and Pakistani women to speak English. There are people who set up play schemes for urban kids, taking them for outings in the country and trips to the seaside.

I have mentioned the white separatist groups like the National Front. Many young blacks are joining a sect called the Rastafarians who preach segregation from whites, they don't believe in mixed marriages. They feel that black kids should be taught more about Africa, especially Ethiopia which they claim is their ancestral home. They worship the late Emperor of Ethiopia Haile Salassie. The followers of this group are easily identified by their hairstyles: the men wear their hair in long ringlets that they call *dread locks* and the women usually wear a turban type wrap on their heads. They have their own kind of music known as *reggae*. This music is popular with both black and white, young and old. Bob Marley, the well known reggae singer did a lot to popularize the Rasta movement in Britain. Songs like 'Crazy Baldheads' and 'No Woman No Cry' were written by Marley who paved the way for other Rasta singers like Eddie Grant and Gregory Isaacs.

The Rastas have developed their own kind of slang words. People who do not agree with them are called *bald heads*. Black girls are known as *daughters* or *beef* and white women are called *the pork*. The *Dub* seems to have a lot of different meanings to them, they seem to use it in a lot of different contexts. The Rastas are the bane of many black parents' lives because they seem to hold a fascination for many of their kids. A lot of black kids who were doing well at school, looking forward to their exams and college, suddenly started to grow their hair in dread locks and started to wear the Rasta colours of red, green and gold. These kids felt that they could identify with the Rastas because the majority of Rastas were young people not much older than themselves. The Movement told the kids what they wanted to hear, mainly that Britain was 'Babylon' which they said 'Jah' (God) would destroy. They were told to drop out, to leave the rat-race to the white man. Every Rastaman's ambition is to go to Ethiopia to live in the ancestral home.

I have been asked if I have any hope of things improving in the future. I must admit that at the moment my immediate thoughts are of trying to make it somewhere else, like America. But on the other hand, I ask myself, would it be fair to uproot my kids from their country and take them to a country like America which is notorious for its racial prejudice? I sometimes feel this might be jumping out of the frying pan into the fire. I feel certain that the recession has a lot to do with the intolerance people seem to be feeling towards each other and if we could just see it through together we might have a chance of making it. If blacks and whites are to live together in harmony they'll have to have a change of ideas on both sides. Those black kids who go around mugging old ladies and thinking they can always get something for nothing will have to realise that they are doing more harm than good, to themselves and the black community as a whole. Many older white people will also have to change their attitudes to blacks and other minority groups. They have to stop thinking of Britain as the Britannia who ruled the waves, they have to realize that the days of the Empire are gone forever. I feel that the day these people can look on black people not as immigrants but as British we'll be a lot nearer to living in peace and harmony together.

Questions

1 Theresa McLean's comments on the experience of being black in Britain raise a number of important issues. Perhaps the first issue to consider is why such terms as 'nigger', 'wog', 'coon' and 'spade' are used to describe people of a colour other than 'white'. Why are such terms used, and what do they tell us about the users?

2 How do you think you would feel towards certain people who only related to you on the basis of your colour? Do you feel that your colour says anything about you as a person; if so, what?

3 What sort of assumptions, if any, would you expect to be made about you on the basis of your colour or your nationality? Would any such assumptions have any validity at all?

4 If you were to go and live in a foreign land, do you think you would choose to live among other people from your country who were living there, or would you rather live among the native majority to whom you were an outsider? Think carefully about your answers and give the reasons for your choice.

5 If you found yourself or your family insulted because you were a 'foreigner', how would you feel about the people who insulted you, and would it affect your attitude towards the majority of the people among whom you were living?

6 Are there any differences between 'black' and 'white' immigrants as far as you are concerned? If so, what are they and in what respects are their experiences of this country likely to differ?

7 Reference is made to Rastas calling women 'daughters', 'beef' and 'pork'. What does this suggest about their attitude to women?

Paul Bogle

The Rastafarian movement and black youth in Britain

David Sparks

David Sparks was born in London during 1940 and evacuated to Paignton, Devon, in 1941. At the age of 15 he enlisted into the army, first serving at the Army Apprentice School, Chepstow, where he met African and Burmese trainees who influenced much of his future thinking on racial issues. He served a further nine years with the Royal Engineers and went overseas to the Southern Cameroons, Hawaii, Aden and other countries during the period of decolonialisation.

In 1962 he married a Jamaican, Thelma McKenzie, and now has two daughters, Marcia and Dionne, aged 23 and 19. On leaving military service, he spent nine years with the Department of Employment, and during that time he became involved in work with black voluntary organisations. In 1976 he was appointed a community relations officer in Waltham Forest, and in 1983 he became the first race relations adviser to that London borough.

Black youth in Britain

There has been a substantial amount of research done on the needs and problems of black youth in Britain. Many views have been presented concerning the problems with which they are confronted. Some of them I will mention in order that some understanding can be had of their situation.

1 A number of black youths were born in the West Indies and were brought up by grandmothers or other relatives, eventually joining their parent or parents in Britain, probably seeing them for the first time in many years and having hardly any knowledge of them. They are then presented with the problem of forming a relationship with their parent(s), possibly a step-parent and step-brothers and sisters as well. They experience difficulty in coming to terms with the new relationships of family, school, British urban community life etc, and as a result of being uprooted, there is occasionally conflict in some of these relationships, if not all.

2 Many adult West Indian immigrants had little choice but to accept low status and low wage employment on arrival in the past and still tend to be employed in low status occupations today. The effect of this on black youth is demoralizing, sometimes causing them to have less respect for their parents who they may see as accepting the situation without protest.

3 For many years there has been hardly any input into the school curriculum which relates positively to black people. Only recently have some schools taken the initiative of ensuring that the curriculum reflects positive images with which the black child can identify. The concern and application to meet this need will vary widely between L E A's and schools. In schools where no provision exists, where the black child receives no information on black heroes in history, social studies etc, there is a danger of the child developing a low self-image. This often can lead to lack of aspirations and stimulation to learn, sometimes manifesting itself in under-achievement.

4 Black youths are experiencing great difficulty in securing employment, particularly employment of interest to them or in the professions. Recent statistics show that there are four times as many unemployed proportionally as white youths.

5 There is a poor relationship between black youths and the police. They feel that the police victimize them. Several at some time during their teenage life come into conflict with the law. Many were charged as a 'suspected person' under Section 4 of the Vagrancy Act, 1824 and found guilty on the sole evidence of the police. In 1977 2,366 persons were arrested in the Metropolitan Police District under this Act of which 1,042 (44%) were black and 1,197 (50%) were white. The Act has now been repealed and replaced.

6 Black youths, through the media (newspapers, TV, radio phone-in etc) are constantly barraged with issues concerning immigration, usually in a derogatory manner. Being the children of immigrants they will take this personally. They meet discrimination and racial abuse in the community.

7 Most of the West Indian community are settled in inner city areas and face the urban deprivation of those areas. In Waltham Forest, according to the 1981 Census, the population in private households with a head born in the Caribbean is 12,776 (6%) and for the New Commonwealth and Pakistan as a whole, 17.5%: the ninth highest proportion in Greater London and the eleventh highest nationally.

Above I have mentioned a few of the situations that effect black youths living in Britain, most of which in one way or another alienate them from the mainstream of British society. Although often born, or having spent most of their life in the UK, many do not feel a true sense of belonging and find a need to fill this vacuum by seeking an identity which is exclusively about being black. In search of something to fulfil this need, a socio-religious movement originating from Jamaica like *Rastafarianism* is an obvious attraction. A movement that is not class-ridden, it embraces those black youths who do not necessarily fit into the more formal and established pattern of life. Furthermore, Rastafarianism appeals to black youths, frustrated and alienated, in that it was born out of protest by the Black World and its inception was at the peak of the colonial period.

Brief history of Rastafarianism
To understand the birth of Rastafarianism, it is best viewed against the history of Jamaica and the black population's struggle for dignity and human rights.

The first protest and revolt against white oppression in Jamaica was made in the 15th century by runaway slaves who became known as the Maroons and the Coromantees (mainly Fanti and Ashanti from what is now Ghana). They produced strong fighting leaders like Cudjoe, Cofi and Acheampong Nanny, a woman, all of whom have become Jamaican folklore heroes. The British regiments were unable to defeat the Maroons and a Peace Treaty was made on 1st March 1738 resulting in the Maroons becoming free and holding land in Cockpit Country and the Blue Mountains.

Another rebellion occurred in 1831 when slaves believing a rumour that abolition had arrived but was being withheld by the Jamaican authorities revolted in their thousands. It was eventually crushed and Sam Sharpe, an outspoken black orator, was executed with many other slaves.

After the abolition of slavery in 1834, the freed slaves realized little comfort from their freedom and found themselves in a situation of forced labour with a pittance for wages. Again this came to a head at Morant Bay in 1865. A wealthy Mulatto, George W Gordon, had been championing the black cause and their socio-economic needs. His friend, a black Baptist preacher, Paul Bogle, took 200 men to protest outside Morant Bay Court House and after an incident some policemen were assaulted. Later when police went to arrest Bogle, a revolt was sparked off, turning that part of the island into turmoil. Many plantations were burnt before the rebellion was put down. Paul Bogle was hanged from the yard-arm of HMS Wolverins and Gordon was hanged at Morant Bay Court House. As many as a thousand others were killed.

Throughout the remainder of the 19th century and into the 20th century, the black population struggled against abject poverty in a class-ridden society with privilege mainly based on the lightness of one's complexion.

The embryo of Rastafarianism developed with Marcus Garvey, a Jamaican, during the 1920's. Garvey's influence grew in the USA. He saw Africa as the black man's salvation and saw a fraternity of the black race, encouraging American blacks to return to Africa. He organized the Universal Negro Improvement Association which had a massive following in the USA.

It was from this background that Rastafarianism developed. Garvey said 'Look to Africa for the crowning of a black King, he shall be the Redeemer'. In 1930 this, in the minds of some, was fulfilled when Haile Selassie became Negus of Ethiopia, King of Kings, Lion of the House of Judah. The scene was set for the formation of a new religious sect. It is an interesting coincidence that 'the redeemer' should have come from Ethiopia. Ethiopia had been an essential element within many of the black Christian sects that had grown in the USA and West Indies. They had interpreted the Bible to relate to the black person. They had put much emphasis on certain passages such as Jeremiah 13, verse 23, 'Can the Ethiopian change his skin, or the leopard his spots?'. Psalm 68, verse 31, 'Princes shall come out of Egypt, Ethiopia and shall soon stretch out her hands unto God'. In a sense Rastafarianism has taken this one step further and adapted the Bible directly to black people, making it significant to them.

Some aspects of the belief and customs of Rastafarianism
Because it is a relatively new religious movement, it is difficult to provide an exact definition. There is variance in practice between Rastafari in Jamaica, Britain, USA etc, and within those communities. However, broadly speaking, some of the following are likely to be practised by Rastafarians:

1 Acceptance of Haile Selassie as the living God (Rastafari).
2 That meat should not be eaten, particularly pork.
3 That they believe in the brotherhood of man but that their first regard is to the sons of Ham (blacks), that they should be charitable to all mankind but firstly toward a fellow Rastafarian.
4 That they follow the ancient laws of Ethiopia.
5 That they should not accept advantages from those who are not Rastafarians.
6 They should be resolute in their love for Rastafari.
7 They should respect other's worship but observe no other god but Rastafari.
8 They should not cut their hair or trim their beards and their head should be covered.
9 That eventually they will return to Ethiopia (some interpret this as Africa as a whole). That they will leave Babylon — (the world of white oppression which includes Jamaica, the Western World).
10 That blacks are in no way inferior to whites.
11 That blacks are the reincarnation of ancient Israel (the holy lands which include Egypt and Ethiopia), who are in exile in other parts of the world.
12 Basically they follow the moral principles of the ten commandments.
13 That marijuana (ganja) is the holy herb. To justify this, Rastafarians use the bible: Genesis 1, verse 12, 'And the earth brought forth grass and herbs yielding seed after his kind, and God saw that it was good'.

Proverbs 15, verse 17, 'Better is a dinner of herb where love is, than a stalled ox and hatred therewith'. Psalm 104, verse 14, 'He causeth the grass to grow for the cattle, and the herb for the service of man'.

It is reasonable to assume from the above that Rastafarianism is not anti-white, it is anti those who oppress black people including fellow blacks and browns. It does encourage pride in being black, which offsets the negative images presented in the past and present.

Two questions that will no doubt be raised are: 'How does the death of Haile Selassie affect Rastafarianism?', and 'How will the followers of the faith return to Africa?' To most, the death of Haile Selassie is the passing on from the temporal state of God or King to the spiritual state. There has been an expectation since the inception of the movement that Rastafarians will return to Africa. The hope is always there but coming to terms with the disappointment of not having returned to date has very often been turned to seeking the rights of blacks in their country of exile.

Attitudes towards Rastafarians
For many years in Jamaica the more affluent members of the society showed scorn for the movement which developed in the slum areas, mainly in Kingston. It is only recently that Rastafarianism has become an integral part of the island's culture and history. Therefore most West Indian parents who left the island before it had gained some respectability hold the old opinions. Many black parents become very concerned when they see their sons and daughters being attracted to the movement. Some black youths seeking a black identity, a black religion, in a race-conscious society will find themselves in conflict with their parents over their involvement with Rastafarianism.

Many white members of our community who are unfamiliar with black youth may feel insecure about dread locks or natty dreads, and about the style of language etc. They will not be aware of the 'peace and love' aspect of the movement, and lack of knowledge leads to fear and prejudice.

The attitude of black youth varies. Some are true believers of Rastafari, others partial believers, probably adorning themselves with the outward signs and practising some aspect of the religion; others have little to do with it, but even these are likely to show sympathy with the movement.

The institutions (schools, employers, government agencies etc) so far seem to have little or no understanding of the movement. They show hardly any acceptance of Rastafarians and give them no credibility. Some schools in the GLC area have allowed girls to cover their heads with scarfs, (but not usually allowing red, green and gold) on presentation of a letter from their parents. Few schools, however, have taken this initiative. Likewise, employers tend to be put off by their appearance, regardless of their ability and keeness to secure employment.

Cultural contribution
Rastafarian culture has manifested itself in Jamaica and prevails in Britain.

Many impressive works of art have been created by Ras Dan Heartman and other Rastafarians, symbolising the roots in Africa and not the imported European culture that influenced much of Jamaica's art previously. Ras Canute and the like have done works of sculpture. Poets such as Sam Brown have produced poetry which illustrates the struggle and poverty in which black people are forced to live. Some of their works also speak out for the Rastafarian faith, and the protest of the black world.

Rastafarians have greatly influenced the music of Jamaica which now has a thriving business in reggae record sales. Some artists like Bob Marley have become household words, not only in the black community but white too. There are hundreds, if not thousands, of other musicians and song writers whose works represent Rastafarian reggae or are influenced by it. The Jamaican Government, during the 'Manley Era', saw Rastafarian art and culture as an enrichment and encouraged it.

Conclusion
The information throughout this piece has given the reader only a glimpse of Rastafarianism. It is hoped, however, that it will provide readers with a more positive understanding of the need that some black youths find to look towards Rastafarianism to counteract the effects of living in a predominantly white society.

Further Reading
The Rastafarians, Leonard E Barrett
Black Mother, Basil Davidson
Death Struggles of Slavery, Henry Bleby
The Philosophy and Opinions of Marcus Garvey, Amy J Garvey
African Fundamentalism, Marcus Garvey
The Ethiopian Church, Isaac Ephriam
The Fighting Maroons of Jamaica, Carey Johnson
White Over Black, Winthrop Jordan

Questions

1 What famous black people in history are you aware of? What are they famous for?
2 Why are so few black people named in history books? What reasons can you think of to explain why black people have been neglected by historians?
3 Do you find any of the beliefs or customs of the Rastafarians any more

strange than the beliefs and customs of any other religion? Give reasons for your opinion.

4 After reading this piece, what do you feel the Rastafarian movement has to offer young black people in Britain? Besides its religious aspects, what other contributions has it made to the culture of Britain?

The delight and the despair

Picture Special By JACK KAY

Glory smile from javelin girl Tessa Sanderson...but for Steve Ovett only sympathy from rival Seb Coe, silver medallist in the 800 metres

Tessa strikes gold as sickness hits Steve

Kathy Cook: New race

A GOLDEN smile from javelin girl Tessa Sanderson, and the dull ache of defeat for Steve Ovett.

In these pictures are the delight and despair of Britain's most successful day ever at Olympic track and field events.

Tessas' medal came on top of a silver for Sebastian Coe in the 800 metres and bronze for Tessa's friendly rival in the javelin, Fatima Whitbread, for Kathy Cook in the

From DAVID EMERY and LEON SYMONS in Los Angeles

400 metres and for Mike McLeod in the 10,000 metres —all within three hours.

But while these Britons headed for the rostrum, Steve Ovett, iron-willed but leaden-lunged and leaden-footed, was being taken on a stretcher to hospital.

Steve stayed on his feet long enough after finishing last in the 800 metres to receive a pat and a word of comfort and sympathy from Seb Coe.

Then, watched by his wife, Rachael, the former world-beater collapsed in the exit tunnel gasping for breath — a victim of hyper-ventilation brought on by a mixture of Los Angeles smog and medicine he had taken for a bronchial complaint.

Unaware of the drama, the other Britons celebrated their success.

Tessa, the Wolverhampton girl who has struggled with tendon problems following

her heartbreak failure to qualify for the Moscow finals, said :

"This is just the greatest moment of my life. I couldn't believe I was watching the Union Jack and hearing the National Anthem all for me."

Throw

She spared a thought for Fatima, too. "I was praying for her to bang in a big throw and win the silver—if not the gold !"

Tessa puzzled millions of TV viewers who heard her say : "The eagle has landed."

It was a private code of thanks to her boss and sponsor, Mr Barrie Whitford, managing director of a Leeds video making company, Television TV.

Tessa, 28, moved to Leeds 14 months ago when Mr Whitford backed her with a secretarial job with time off for training plus a £20,000-a-year package in sponsorship and salary.

Kathy Cook, the 24-year-old housewife who, like Tessa, comes from Wolverhampton, is planning further success as she's also running in the 200 metre event.

ALL THE OLYMPIC ACTION — PAGES 34-36 : EXPRESS OPINION — PAGE 8

Feeling the difference
M A S Lawla

A Londoner, British born of Jamaican parents, Mark Lawla is twenty years old and at present a VDU operator with an accountancy college. He completed A level studies in Mathematics and English at the Islington Sixth Form Centre and Central Foundation Boys' School last year, and has since worked as a bookshop assistant with a high street chain and also with his present employers. With several poems printed in the Caribbean Times and The Voice, he describes himself as an 'occasional scribbler' and a Bob Marley fan.

Feeling the difference was first given live testing at the Hackney based Jenako Arts Centre and several improvements to the text were made possible by the feedback of members.

Slip into the image that isn't ours?
Never can be, never shall be;
For whose harmony must we ourselves deny?
Ours? Yours? The Community as one?
No — surely not ours . . .
For should we forget the shade we're in
(With minds neatly laundered of that 'awareness' thing)
There are always reminders of society's thinking
Telling us we're apart, not a part, of its thinking:

The Fleet Street Black a thug in an alley
Blacker than black, the alien in jeans,
The Fleet Street Black a sporting delight
Sweating for Britain aptly more pale.

In one the pride, in another the pain
That should not be felt in the link of skin
For really, aren't we British all?
So the myth is sent along
Physical prowess labelled grace, labelled wrong.

The great amnesia of schooled thought
Gives nothing to fight the lies,
Nothing to note of Our past achievement

(We had no past to speak of)
Nothing of Our culture Our people —
We all share the common history
Of the poor, oppressed, pissed up on Black;
We are taken in to renounce our kin
While a stillborn reason lies uneasy.

'The minority has no right to impose itself,
Must succumb to survive, bear integration's burden,
We shall make no compromise. No concession —'
(The belief: we should eat our chips not shoulder them).

So it seems but then what hope for peace?
Our sense of identity cannot be lost,
Force of fact or positive will impresses,
OUR ROOTS MUST STAY FIRM —
Smash self-respect and anger soothes despair
As our souls are bleached, and 'blackness' preached.

Have you heard the one about . . .?
Donal Carroll

Donal Carroll was born in the Republic of Ireland. He has had various jobs including television engineering in Dublin and London. He attended Fircroft College, Birmingham and Warwick and Essex Universities, and taught at Norwich City College, Clare College, Cambridge, and Hounslow Borough College, London. He has written books, articles and reviews and poetry for a variety of magazines, including Don't you believe it!, *(a further education text); an article on the rise of skills in FE for the* NATFHE *Journal of Further and Higher Education; and contemporary poetry reviews for* City Limits. *He is at present working on the cabaret circuit as a comedian and poet, and has also appeared on radio and television. His poetry is appearing in anthologies from Pluto Press and from Chatto and Windus in 1985—6.*

You've heard the one about the Irishman who tried to get helicopters to land in his garden by leaving out breadcrumbs, but have you heard about the Irish Evil Kneivel? Well, he is going to jump over ten English people using a steamroller and he's made three unsuccessful attempts already. The second joke sounds like a desperate example of retribution. In that case, what is the first joke an example of?

Traditionally, jokes reveal the relationship between the teller and the target. Of course nobody actually *believes* that the Irish are inferior; that would be taking it too far. People cracking jokes never would, never *could* prove their case through jokes, but they certainly can universalize their *tone*. (Tone is the soft wrapping round the brick you're throwing.) Look at the assumptions which automatically follow Irish jokes like these. What did the Irishman say when he was caught stealing housebricks? 'Ah, sure, I was going to bring them back when I was finished with them'. Why does an Irishman wear three Durex? To be sure, to be sure, to be sure. P.S. they're worn on his thumb. The Irish are dull, intensely stupid, forever falling off their tongues.

So, as an Irishman, being on the receiving end of these jokes is difficult in literal terms. Sometimes not laughing causes bad feeling and accusations of being mean-spirited or not being able to take a joke. You can't neutralize the jokes by, for example, substituting the word 'Englishman' in any Irish jokes. It won't work. It will not work for the

IRISH ARCHITECTURE.

Angler (in Ireland). "Hullo, Pat, what are you about now?"
Pat. "Shure, I'm Raisin' me Roof a bit, yer Honour-r!!"

same reason that you cannot substitute the word 'man' in the following joke: Did you hear about the woman with five legs? Her knickers fitted like a glove. Like I said, there's something in the patronizing wrapping, the tone; something in the assumed relationship between the teller and the target, the receiver. If that assumption is not present, the joke ceases to exist.

Taking the jokes literally, would mean asking for space to quantify what's left out, deliberately missing. Didn't Yeats, Synge, O'Casey, Wilde, Shaw etc make contributions to English language and culture? Why did they not fit into the pattern of being Irish?

So re-uniting tone and content, I have taken to being insulting by reply. Have you heard about the Irishman who . . . 'No', I interrupt 'Is it true your wife left you because she always had to start without you?' Or 'How's the hernia transplant?' Or 'Is it true you used to take in washing before they found you out?' (This is not a question.) My, my, but *why* does he have to be so insulting? Like I said, it's all in the tone.

For immigrants, though, the real pain lies not only in what is left unsaid, but in the political ramifications behind the 'humour'. For years we had the jokes about the Jews, then, in the late sixties about Pakistanis and West Indians, then, through the seventies about homosexuals and the Irish. This latter is certainly connected with the emergence, yet again, of the Irish Problem. Everybody wishes it would go away, but ignoring it on the mainland for the last four hundred years has not succeeded in making it go away and it certainly won't now either. The jokes hide a colossal historical ignorance. Not necessarily of Ireland's history but of Britain's role in it. Ask anybody cracking Irish jokes where did Northern Ireland come from, or was there anything democratic about its appearance, or much more fundamentally, who is responsible for the maintenance of this state of ignorance? Answers on the back of a stamp, please. The briefest of glances at Irish history (Oh God, he's not getting political is he? After all it was only a joke!) will reveal plenty of evidence of racialism. It has quite a respectable pedigree too. Edmund Spenser, sixteenth century poet and author of *The Fairie Queen*, in advancing British policy in Ireland, where he was chief clerk of Munster, advocated the extermination of his neighbours. He referred to Munster, a beautiful southern province, where he lived and was married, as 'monster'. Sir Walter Raleigh, known throughout Britain for throwing capes over troubled waters, had such a fierce, genocidal reputation in Cork county that his name is still used as a bogeyman to frighten children. As for Oliver Cromwell, the less said the better. Over in Ireland, that is. And these are just historical hors-d'oeuvres.

The form might have changed, but the antipathy is nothing new. Listen to this:

'A creature manifestly between the gorilla and the negro is to be met in some of the lowest districts of London and Liverpool by adventurous explorers. It comes from Ireland, whence it has contrived to migrate, it belongs in fact to the tribe of Irish savages; the lowest species of the Irish Yahoo. When conversing with its kind, it talks a sort of gibberish. It is, moreover, a climbing animal, and may sometimes be seen ascending a ladder laden with a hod of bricks.'

This 'humorous' portrait is taken from *Punch* of 1862. There was an Irish Problem then too. It is reflected in the tone. They were clearly making a nuisance of themselves. Equality, Emancipation, Home Rule, Enfranchisement, that sort of thing. Unforgiveable. And most decidedly unBritish.

Immigrants have always been in the position of exchanging the cap in hand of their own country for the cash in hand of the next. This is true of *all* immigrants. The Irish are the largest immigrant group in Britain because of the nearness of the two islands and because of their willingness to be among the first wage slaves. This economic connection means they are not just something marginal but are at the very core of politics, as with all migrant workers. The Irish are also, per capita, amongst the most organized. (Engels actually thought that the 'passionate, mercurial Irish temperament' would soften 'the cold, rational English character'.) Their only recognised difference from natives is their capacity for a long day's blarney into night. Historically denied social and political freedom, the freedom of the tongue is all they have been allowed. The systematic destruction of their own language and culture is the social basis for this 'if-words-were-wages-we'd-all-be-millionaires'; it's really a form of social laryngitis. And people tend to listen to the music not the meaning. Needless to say, the problem is not one limited to Ireland.

Given this immensely long arm of history, the jokes are simply a continuation and should be seen as anti-Irish. 'Ignorance' is as good a term in that those who do not know history are doomed to re-live it.

There are twelve million migrant workers in western Europe. The advent of the EEC will mean more strangers in the High Street, each carrying their own history and introducing the average British bypass-dweller to theirs.

So, the next time you're in the saloon bar sitting down to a pint and some roast beef (probably Irish) and Surrey pudding and you announce 'Did you hear about the Irishman who . . .', don't be surprised if a white immigrant interrupts you with 'How do you make an Irishwoman pregnant?' You don't know? And you call *them* stupid?

Tone
Donal Carroll

Dinner parties;
all windows, no doors:
vision vesseling:
Bubble and squeak and boiling teeth:
Can you cohear me!

She treats the knives and forks like jewellery.
Her voice is marinated in the social juices,
class-clinking, leaking that confidence
that suggests growth.

'The trouble with this country
is there's too much equality . . .
'you know' is added,
the syringe which breaks the skin.

'Equality? I suppose that's why the House of Lords
discusses overmanning in industry . . .

'Oh you must be Irish . . . such a charming race of nomads;
so suited to poetry; the Amuse breaking sweat.
All that rustic charm; towing peat and nettles
by horse, the cart with model T exhaust pipe;
the banshees wailing into their homegrown Gaelic coffee:
haven't you passed pastoral yet?
Your gravid writers, blinded by Mother Guiness,
snipped in the bud . . . Ulsterectomy, I believe.
Do pass the syllabub.'
'No.
Yes, we've learned well from the Master Culture:
content is something mugged by opportunity;
statement is something meant to state at least its opposite;
public concern is always on a different channel, only in mono;
effect, cause and symptom are all the same, and only symptons are
moral;
the writer's conscience is an oxymoron.
Yes, politics is a stockinged-foot invader; it just pollutes
the decorative stroking of the ego. The best poetry, in fact,

is a cross between a fridge and a bank. Chilled and safe.
As for Ireland, why not tow it out 1000 miles into the Atlantic
and call it Chile; much easier to ignore.

What exactly convinces you there is any life
on this island that can't be traced
to us immigrants?'

'You can't be serious!
Is that a question??'

'No. A refrain.
When did you last make a decision?'

'A what?'

'Decision.
The state of siege between
termination and reverberation.'

'Oh but we never make decisions.
We're Surrealists!!'

'What does that mean . . . You're from Surrey . .'

Questions

Have you heard the one about . . .?
1 Donal Carroll's article concentrates on the Irish as the butt of jokes
   about the immigrant in Britain. Who are the other targets for
   'immigrant' jokes?
2 Are all jokes against races or nationalities told from a position of
   superiority on the part of the teller? Do you know of any jokes that are
   about a group of people who are supposed to be superior to the person
   telling the joke?
3 What purpose do jokes told against a section of the population have? Is
   the 'humour' merely a cloak to cover the hostility of the host country
   towards the immigrant, or are there other things involved?
4 Donal Carroll makes a convincing case for the serious implications of
   ethnic jokes, suggesting that they work to trivialize oppression and
   prejudice. What do you think about this?
5 Write down an example of an ethnic joke, then analyse the
   implications behind it. What assumptions are there about the people
   who are the butt of the joke, and what assumptions are made about the
   people who will laugh at it?
6 Many tribes or nationalities tell jokes about other tribes or
   nationalities. See if you can find out who people of other cultures tell
   jokes about, then see if their jokes have anything in common with the
   British variety.

Tone

1 What is the main feeling that the writer seems to have towards the people described in this poem, and what sort of people are they?
2 What is this poem trying to express?
3 What does this poem have in common with the two poems preceding it?
4 What are the things that you dislike most about this country, and what are the things that you most like about it? Perhaps you could write a poem on the subject.

A Kenyan Asian in Britain
Rahila Alam

Rahila Alam is 21. She was born in Pakistan, but lived in Kenya for eleven years, emigrating to England at the age of 11. Since then, she has continued her education in England, and has taken her A level examinations at Windsor and Maidenhead College in Berkshire. Resident in Slough, Berkshire, she is studying for a Bsc Sociology degree at the University of Leicester, after which she hopes to embark on a career in personnel management.

On the 25th of May 1975, a great change took place in my life and it brought with it new experiences, problems and ideas. I distinctly remember my arrival in England from Kenya, the country in which I spent my early childhood, where Swahili was the mother tongue.

It was about three o'clock in the afternoon when the plane landed and as I descended from it, a strange feeling overcame me. As I looked around, everything seemed very different. The weather was so gloomy and cold, even the air seemed to possess a peculiar smell, which perhaps was due to the rain. Most people happened to be wearing jeans, which would have been thought unusual in Kenya unless perhaps one was going to safari or on an outing of a similar kind.

Even on entering the airport, I still had that strange feeling inside me for the atmosphere was completely different. I felt eyes glaring at me. This, I think, was solely due to feelings of self-consciousness, as I appeared to be so different to the majority of the people. However, whilst looking around, I was comforted by the presence of some people who had a similar complexion to mine and this made me feel less of an outcast.

However, in times to come, I realized that it was not only the colour of my complexion that was different but that other more important and complex differences existed as well. I became aware of most of these when I commenced school at the age of eleven. I was amazed at the differences between my school in England and the one on Kenya. The attitudes of the children and teachers differed greatly. I was surprised at the degree of freedom children were privileged to have, to wear what they desired and express their feelings quite freely, whereas in Kenya uniform was compulsory and freedom of speech was not really permitted in schools. We, in a way, were compelled to agree with the teachers and

not argue with them or question them, or we would face punishment. Punishment took the form of caning. I admire this freedom in an English school, as I think a child is encouraged to be more creative and be able to form his or her own ideas, something on which I probably lost out in the early years.

I happened to go through what at the time seemed to be a few embarrassing situations but which, when I look back at them, appear to be quite trivial or funny. In a Kenyan school we were told to always greet a teacher politely and formally whenever we met one. Thus, obviously, when I started school in England, I greeted every teacher that I passed with a cheerful 'Good morning'. This, however, in an English middle-school did not elicit a very favourable response. I noticed peculiar facial expressions being made by others and I was soon made a laughing-stock. To be quite truthful, I found my early days in an English school quite miserable and depressing. This was probably due to me becoming aware of differences that I had never thought of before.

In the early days, I suffered some racial discrimination, being called a 'Paki' and other such names. I did not find names such as 'Paki' offensive in themselves, as truthfully I am proud to be a Pakistani, it is just the way in which they were shouted and the feelings and thought implied behind them, that offended me. At that particular time, I must admit, I began to detest the host country and its community. However, this feeling changed as years passed by and I grew older and became accustomed to English ideas. I understood that all that had been silly ignorant kids' talk.

Apart from these minor racial tensions, there were other problems that arose which did not solely apply to me, but also applied to others who came from a similar, foreign background to mine.

School dinners caused problems, as the dinner at that time was a set meal everyday and, as many people know, Muslims are not permitted to eat pork. The meat of any other animal can only be eaten if it is 'kosher' meat. This caused problems as many of us could not have school dinners and had to settle for sandwiches instead of perhaps a hot meal, the other alternative being to run home.

Personally, I also found it difficult to follow certain subjects such as history. Everything was based on Christianity or British culture and British history, and as I had only a passing knowledge of these subjects I always found it difficult to contribute in these lessons.

As I grew older and commenced secondary school I realized that I had two different personalities. I was now familiar with the English way of life but even more aware of my differences. I would adopt English ideas at school or when out of the house, and got on quite well with people of the host community. However, as soon as I returned home, I had to play a completely different role in a constrasting culture.

My parents are not as strict as parents of many other Muslim people; however they still hold on to their ideas and values and most of these, I must add, are cultural and not religious.

In an Asian family, everything is centred on religion, culture and the family itself. Respect and the reputation of the family are very important to all Asians and they generally tend to go to any extremes to keep them even if many sacrifices have to be made. One of the main examples here is that of arranged marriages. In my religion, Islam, an arranged marriage is not compulsory. However, many people are forced into them as these ideas were adopted many years ago and the tradition is still pursued. Even though this custom is now deteriorating slowly with many youngsters rebelling against it, it still holds an important place and is a controlling force in Asian society. Parents are supposed to choose an appropriate husband for the girl, or an appropriate wife for the boy. The grandparents and other relatives usually have to be consulted before this step is taken. Some choice is allowed to the boy or the girl to choose his or her partner but this varies from family to family. In some cases, a girl may be shown just a photograph of the man that she is supposed to marry and she does not have much say in the matter, whereas, in other cases, the girl is allowed to choose a husband from a number of men that have been selected by her parents. The same applies to boys. However, the wishes of the parents must be obeyed, otherwise the reputation of the family will suffer. This statement is thrust upon any male or female who wishes to do otherwise.

Arranged marriages often tend to be successful but there are cases where problems occur, due to two people having different ideas or interests. However, they continue to be married, despite the conflict, to prevent the family reputation from suffering.

Boys tend to be given more freedom in socializing as it is considered that their reputation is not affected as much as a girl's is and, therefore, Asian parents tend to be very cautious in allowing their daughters certain kinds of freedom. Some will go to the extremes of not allowing their daughter to work or go out anywhere without them.

This might appear very strange to the people of the host community, but they will only fully understand the importance of family respect and reputation if they understand the values and morals of the Asian community and realize the consequences suffered by the individual if these values are distorted or rejected — a total rejection from the family.

Western culture I find to be a complete contrast. I perceive it to be a less close-knit community, an individual being permitted much more freedom to do what he or she thinks is right and this is helped by the different values and morals that the British have.

These differences created barriers as, even though I had become accustomed to English ideas, I was unable to fully adopt them due to the many physical and psychological restrictions and pressures placed upon me. Many of my friends failed to understand why I was not allowed out very often and never fully understood my culture and its values, thus, they often criticized them. Therefore, in my opinion, one of the main barriers to racial harmony is the one of not comprehending the morals and the values of other cultures. Perhaps a clear understanding of each other's culture would lead to a closer link between communities and an acceptance of each other's way of life.

One of the methods by which a closer link could be formed between different communities is through the education system. Education should be based on a variety of cultures, rather than just the Western way of life. This will be a help to all communities. They will learn about other cultures but at the same time not lose out in examinations which may be biased towards Christianity or Western ideas.

Also, perhaps a system should be provided for people who are unable to speak English, whereby they could attend such functions as parents' evenings without too much worry. I agree that people should learn the host language; however, this will come slowly as the mother tongue is the most important and should be learnt first. I have made this point about language as I have come across many Asian parents who tend to ignore such functions as parents' evenings due to feeling inferior or ashamed of not being able to speak English. Furthermore, it would be pointless for the parents to attend these functions if they were unable to communicate with people, or teachers, in the case of parents' evenings. It appears that some Asian parents do not fully understand the education system and this leads to a lack of interest in the child's education. This is a major drawback, as the child seems not to be encouraged enough and may lose interest in education.

To look upon the whole issue of racial difference realistically, it would appear that the only way in which different communities can live in harmony is through mutual respect.

Questions

1 What are the first differences that Rahila Alam notices between Britain and Kenya?
2 What problems does she experience at school as a result of her Pakistani origins?
3 How might such problems be diminished in the future?
4 What are some of the differences described between Asian culture and that of the West?
5 What suggestions does Rahila Alam make that would help bridge the gap between the two cultures?
6 What do you think of her suggestions and what suggestions, if any, would you make in addition to them?

A Scottish lion rampant

John Singh

My name is John Singh and I am twenty years of age. My father, who served in the British Army during World War Two, came to this country after the partition of the Punjab in 1947. Like many Sikhs and Hindus who found themselves in the Muslim part he was obliged to flee and spent many months in a refugee camp. My father's name is Rangit but in Glasgow he is known as John. When he came to Glasgow in 1951 he got a job as a driver in Glasgow Transport and after saving for some years went into the taxi business with his brother. They double-shifted their first vehicle until they could afford a second one.

Like all Sikh boys I am named 'Singh' or Lion after one of the ten gurus of our religion. We grow our hair long, do not shave, wear the turban and do not indulge in alcohol or tobacco. All Sikhs should adhere to these customs but some become 'tapit' or lapsed Sikhs. My father has ceased to be orthodox although like most fathers he brings up his family in the strict traditions of our race. Although he has ceased to wear the turban he is still at heart a Sikh. Anyway due to the industry of my father and uncle the family has prospered materially and we own our house even though it is a very old property.

When I was five years old I was sent to school — not a very pleasant experience if you can't speak the language and wear outlandish clothes. We spoke Bengali at home and it was not an advantage to be the only non-European in the class. The other children regarded me as a strange curiosity and my knot of hair became the target for the more aggressive. My father had told me not to fight unless I was first of all attacked and that I should bear any insults without showing anger or resentment. As time went by things gradually improved; I was good at sport, popular with my teachers and quickly picked up the language. Soon I could speak better English than my parents and thought myself superior to my old grandfather who could not speak a word of the new tongue.

When I was twelve I went to secondary school and although we learned new subjects like Algebra and Physics I had to travel further to get there. The school was in Pollokshields, a suburb of Glasgow, once respectable middle class terraced mansions but now mainly an immigrant area. Most of the children were non-European; many Pakistanis, some Sikhs and Hindus and a few Chinese from Hong Kong. The Scottish boys were always the worst behaved in the class room and the biggest bullies outside of it. Most of them had no interest in their lessons, no respect for teachers or parents and most of the time they smoked, gambled or fought in the playground or played truant for weeks on end. Neither myself nor their teachers missed them.

One day a boy two years older than myself struck me because during a game of football in the yard I had taken the ball from him. 'That was a foul, you b . . . . b . . . . . .', he screamed lashing out at me. I lost control of myself and hit him on the chin. He went down in a heap and it was not until he had been carried into the sick-room that he started coming round. The headmaster was very angry and I thought I was certain to be expelled but after several witnesses had stated that I had not started the trouble he calmed down and let me off with a severe reprimand. Should any trouble ever occur I was not to retaliate because I did not know my own strength. If I was in such a situation I was to see him first and not take vengeance into my own hands.

It was around this period that I passed through the Sikh process of initiation. At adolescence boys assume the name Singh and adopt the five Ks. From henceforth their hair and beard remain uncut, they wear their hair coiled under the turban (*Kesh*). At least twice a day they comb their hair with the *Kangha* or comb. On their right wrist they wear a steel bangle (*Kara*) and on ceremonial occasions they dress in the *Katchacha* or soldier's shorts and carry the *Kirpan* or short sabre. Daily they will honour their religion by reading from the Adi Granth or original scriptures, and attend, where possible the Sikh temple or *Gurdwara*. Many Sikhs are vegetarians but increasing numbers of them have ceased to be so through living in Britain and other countries.

When I was sixteen I sat my SCE 'O' Grade examinations and I thought I had performed reasonably well. During the vacation I considered whether to return for further schooling or to take up employment. I wanted to be an asset to my family and there was something grown-up in going out to earn a living. By British standards there are rather a lot of people in our household; there are my parents, my father's parents, my uncle, my three younger brothers and two older sisters. Only my father and uncle are earning money and there are a lot of expenses. My mind was made up, I would take a job.

A firm advertised in the newspaper for apprentice television engineers. Just the thing I thought. I applied and was given an interview. The man I saw was not at all friendly. I could sense that right away. I felt somehow a deeply held hostility. It was not that he said anything but there seemed something sardonic in his cosmetic smile and unnatural politeness. Perhaps it was my turban which upset him because all the time he seemed unable to take his eyes off it. At any rate my worst fears were confirmed because a week later I was informed that I had been unsuccessful in my application. All that long summer was an encore of the same story, 'Sorry the job has been filled'. By this time I had received my examination results. I had passed them all with distinction but there were still no employment prospects and I was reconciled to returning to school. There I would be at least the equal of the other immigrants.

My father, who had been following the course of events got in touch with a friend who was a member of the Race Relations Council. He advised me to apply to the Glasgow District Council whose Housing Department took on young people for apprenticeships. I did as he suggested and soon got an interview. This time it was a woman who interviewed me and she was both friendly and helpful. She asked me why I wanted the job and I explained my family's position. Then there followed an English and Arithmetic test and an aptitude test which involved fitting shapes into a board. I must have created a favourable impression because within a fortnight I started as an electrical apprentice.

This was my first experience of employment and like all beginners I had to go through the initiation of being sent on fool's errands for tins of tartan paint and left-handed screwdrivers. The squad, or at least some semi-literate member, called me Sabu after some character in Kipling's *Jungle Book*, not that they had read it but they might have seen the film. There was nothing nasty or personal in the banter; a Chinese would have been called Charlie Chan or a negro Rastus. It was a form of racialism but one in which the participants did not realize their involvement. To them it was natural that someone with a different pigmentation of the skin should be made aware of it, just like a one-legged man or a hunchback.

I had the job of making the tea, getting the rolls, sandwiches and cigarettes and carrying the tools and equipment. I had this dubious honour not because I was a Sikh but because I was the most recent apprentice and by custom and tradition these were the tasks he performed, perhaps as a means of dispelling any false pride and inducing humility.

As time went on I ceased to be the junior apprentice and got more important work to do; cutting the conduit into the appropriate lengths; screwing the ends for couplings and bending it into the required shapes; making channels through joists and walls for electrical points. It was hard work and often I would return home in the evenings totally exhausted and covered from turban to toe in brick dust and my muscles aching.

I remember one Friday afternoon we broke up early for the Christmas and New Year holidays. It was the custom to go to the public house for a drink. As a Sikh I did not have much to celebrate but I went along and although I did not touch alcohol I took an orangeade. While I was in the toilet some joker must have spiced my drink because shortly afterwards I began to feel uncomfortably warm and uncertain in my movements. Somewhat erratically I made my way home using the lamposts more for support than illumination, singing the warrior songs that I had learned from my grandfather. My father was very angry at my condition and wanted to make a complaint but once I had sobered up I explained that it was an old Scottish custom and that no harm had been intended. Nevertheless I was much more circumspect on future festive occasions.

As part of my apprenticeship training I attended a Further Education College on a one day per week basis. Here we were preparing for the City and Guilds Examination in our trade. Apart from the practical training in the workshop we were taught the theoretical basis of all things electrical and mechanical pertaining to our craft. We also spent time in what was termed, 'English and General Studies' where we were taught how to communicate both orally and on paper and how to express our thoughts with clarity for examination purposes. At least this was the intention although many students preferred to be happy in their ignorance; they considered themselves electricians and not students of language or linguistics.

One day the teacher asked if any of us from the commonwealth (he had a more delicate way of putting things than some others I have met) might be interested in writing an account of our experiences at work and school and how it felt to grow up in what might be considered to be an alien culture. I had up till that point never thought of doing so although I did have, when I came to think about it, definite opinions on the subject.

That is how I came to be writing this article. Other Asian students in the class started off with the same idea but all of them lost interest and dropped out. While the class has continued with their current affairs, memoranda and reports, I have struggled to separate the important from the trivial aspects of life and attempt to impose some coherence upon seemingly random occurrences. I cannot type but the teacher has promised to do this for me while at the same time correcting any spelling or grammatical irregularities but retaining the substance and spirit of my story.

The Scottish way of life is very different from our own. Most people are neither ambitious nor particularly hard-working. Unlike most Sikhs they have no desire to improve themselves. If for example they become unemployed they blame their bad luck or the government; they sign on at the Labour Exchange and complain they don't have enough money. My work mates, who are good fellows, work hard all week and then give most of their money, not to their families, but to the bookies and publicans. They are always, despite being in employment, short of money. It is unusual for the vast majority of them to own their own home or to ever consider setting up their own businesses. When their parents get old they are left to fend for themselves or failing that put into geriatric homes mainly because their sons and daughters are too busy leading their own trivial lives. Most people also have little concern for their children; both parents often work leaving the children to bring themselves up. Parents do not always show their children a good example and if they smoke and swear in the home it is not surprising that their children do likewise. It is not surprising that there is so much crime and juvenile delinquency because in this country what masquerades as 'freedom' is really a definite lack of concern and social control. People here do not realize how lucky they are in having a Welfare State and adequate pensions and allowances. Certainly there is recession and unemployment but there is nothing like the poverty that is found in Bombay or Calcutta. There is great political freedom and a lack of censorship yet most people are apathetic and take everything for granted. They envy the immigrants who come here poor, make a success of their lives and end up owning businesses. Scottish people seem preoccupied with the trivia of life; horse-racing, football pools, bingo and television.

My Scottish friends marry yet they don't seem to take it very seriously because they prefer to spend much of their leisure time in the pub with their mates. Before they marry they knock around with a variety of girls and go to discos and get into fights. In my opinion this seems such an awful waste of time and effort.

As for myself I shall take my father's advice about marriage. In this society people claim to marry for love then spend the rest of their lives getting over their mistakes. I do not like the British customs such as divorce because apart from it being an admission of failure, it is very upsetting for the couple concerned and disastrous for the children.

We Sikhs believe in arranged marriages. Contrary to general belief they are not forced marriages because the couple meet several times to see if they are compatible — so there is no coercion. The family merely arrange that two young people who are apparently suitable should meet because by our custom it is not only the couple who are concerned but their families also. My father says that in a few years I shall probably marry a second cousin who is two years younger than me and who lives in Birmingham. With us it is important that both families live in harmony, that the husband is caring and hard-working and that the wife is prudent and obeys.

I am often asked by British people what it feels like to grow up in a strange country whose customs are vastly different from those of India. I can only say that I know India only through the eyes of my parents and grandparents. As I have grown up here I am quite happy here, probably happier than I would be as a farmer in the Punjab which would be even more of a foreign land to me. What upsets me, although this is becoming less freqeunt, is when strangers appear to take a dislike to me because I am a Sikh and wear a turban and not for any harm I have done them. Once when I was working with a tradesman a woman who wanted a repair done refused to let me into her house. My mate was all for refusing to do the job but I told him not to make a fuss so he completed the job while I sat in the cafe reading the newspaper. Such incidents are few but they are sufficient to cause embarrassment. Some people are initially hostile but once they get to know you sufficiently well their prejudice diminishes and they usually end up seeing you as a human being and not some stereotype of their imagination.

In some places in Britain the National Front and the Skinheads make life difficult for the immigrant community but there is no trouble like that in Glasgow. Perhaps one of the reasons for this that there is already enough hostility already between the rival and bigoted supporters of the 'Old Firm'.

I once went to an Old Firm game between Celtic and Rangers at Ibrox Stadium. A friend of mine who is a Rangers fan invited me to go for what he termed 'a great experience'. Well it was. He gave me a Rangers scarf to wear and for once I left off my turban and put on a red-white-and-blue tammy. I was for the day an unheard of phenomenon — a Sikh Rangers supporter!

Before the game began the fans had assembled on the terracing, were drinking from cans and bottles (which is illegal but still an old Scottish custom). They were singing songs about what I thought was Delhi walls but which my friend corrected me was Derry Walls — a reference, to some historic victory in Ireland — although what it had to do with a football match escaped me. By the time the teams appeared many of the supporters were already drunk and were shouting abuse at the opposing team and their supporters who were confined to the other end of the stadium. Even my friend who was normally very quiet became excited once the game had commenced. Like the rest he started cheering on his own idols and mouthing profanities at the team in green-and-white. When Rangers scored the opening goal, the fans went hysterical, hugging and kissing each other and jumping up and down. Spectators embraced like long lost lovers and hurled their tammies into the air as if to placate the gods. Finally the game ended in a draw and we made our way slowly out of the ground. Already sporadic fighting had broken out and police were arresting fans who were being bodily thrown into the 'black maria' or police wagons and taken away. In India, at the time of partition, about two million people lost their lives but I don't think the Hindus and Muslims could have hated each other to the same extent as those rival football fanatics that I saw that day. If this is sport then I will try something else. Yet strangely enough those same supporters can live and work in harmony in a normal situation.

Each week I put away part of my pay and in a year's time I hope to have saved enough for a deposit for a motorbike. By then I shall, all being well, have completed my apprenticeship and passed my City and Guilds final examination. When I have gained sufficient experience I hope someday to start my own electrical business. I could of course go into the family taxi business but I prefer electrical work to constant driving at all hours of the day and night.

There are few Sikhs in Glasgow who have become tradesmen mainly because by tradition we are warriors and farmers. But we must move with the times and accept that those of us who have left the Punjab have left that way of life and must come to terms with an industrial society. We

Sikhs do not worship money or seek (no pun intended) to exploit others. We are forbidden to deal in commodities like alcohol and tobacco so we cannot become publicans or run licensed grocers or tobacconists. At the same time we have no wish to become parasities upon the host country so we must take up occupations which are honourable and confer dignity. Young Sikhs will in increasing numbers take up trades and professions. At the same time although our ways of earning a living are changing we must, as Sikhs, retain the fundamentals of our philosophy which are to be aware of the dangers of materialism and of pursuing false ideals. It is difficult having to live in the world having to make a living within a society and yet avoid being corrupted by it. We must not be ensnared by Maya or the world of illusion. For us God is one and not as the Hindus believe many. God is present in all things yet is unknowable. He has no attributes yet is everything. We lead this life and continue through the transmigration of souls to seek perfection. When we obtain perfection through *Khalsa* or the brotherhood of the pure our earthly life ceases and we meet God. God can only be found indirectly through the gurus who lead us from darkness into enlightenment. Through the example of the Guru Nanak, the founder of our religion, and the other gurus we learn to tread the path of righteousness.

We Sikhs are a proud people. We do not beg from others. We give generously to charity not only to our own people but to others as well. We have no priesthood and no saints so we must make our own way.

As for politics, most Sikhs remain uninvolved. In my father's opinion this is a mistake because ultimately politics has a bearing on our way of life and the opportunities we have open to us. In immigrant areas such as Garnethill, Govanhill or Pollokshields in Glasgow, Asians standing for election, whether they be Pakistani, Hindu or Sikh would get the immigrant vote, especially if the immigrant community saw itself as being threatened or openly discriminated against. It is now belatedly being recognised that there are not enough Asians entering the police, the armed forces, the civil service and other professions. The time is not far off when the youth shall no longer be content in pursuing their fathers' occupations — the general store keeper and the itinerant market trader.

The immigration laws may also force us into politics. We accept the fears of Mrs Thatcher and her Conservatives that Britain might be 'swamped' by an incursion of immigrants from the sub-continent. What seems very obvious is that tightening up of the laws are aimed only at the Asians; people from Canada, Australia, New Zealand, White Rhodesians and those from the European Community and even Americans seem technically free to come and reside in Britain. This is why immigration to us seems racial rather than rational. Most people in Britain seem unaware that Britain as an imperial power annexed the Punjab by force of arms after the so-called Sikh War of 1842. It was also the British who massacred hundreds at Amritsar in 1919 when General Dyer's troops fired on the crowd.

In 1947 the British left India but the partitioning of the country led to massacre on a massive scale. Not only was India partitioned but the Punjab was split betwen India and Pakistan. It may not have been an intentional blunder but millions were either slaughtered or dispossessed. That was the background to many Sikhs coming to Britain; they came not by choice but because they had lost everything that they valued.

Mr Powell is a bad man in the eyes of many immigrants and British liberals, but he merely says what many British people think. We recognise his honesty although we deplore everything he stands for. He is a very intelligent man but a very warped one and although he claims to have an excellent knowledge of history a few facts seem to have escaped him.

Britain is a country in decline: in population, in industry, in morale. This decline has coincided with a period of immigration and some unthinking people blame immigrants as the cause of it all! That is why the National Front and the so-called British Movement have continued to flourish when they are simply 'front' organizations for racialism and Fascism.

I am a young man brought up in this country but with roots in the old. I see the advantages and disadvantages of both societies and how we can learn from past mistakes. I claim no originality of thought because many of the opinions expressed are composite ones gained through long discussions with my father, uncle, Sikh friends and with students and staff at college. We are what our experiences have made us and as a young man mine have been limited. As I go through life my opinions shall undoubtedly alter although there is no guarantee that experience and age bring wisdom.

I have been concerned here with explaining how it feels to be a Sikh brought up in a western society which is admittedly tolerant but indifferent to the culture of others. Many Britons might say that immigrants, because they choose to come here, should adopt the cultural pattern of the British and should seek assimilation rather than retain their native individuality. To this I can only say that in these small British Isles, the English, the Scots, the Welsh and the Irish have maintained their distinctive linguistic and cultural peculiarities while becoming loosely what is a blanket term — 'British'. Should the immigrants be shown less consideration?

Finally may I conclude by saying we did not come here with a begging bowl like paupers but each with two hands willing to work. The fact that many foreigners like Reo Stakis come over here and become millionaires says much for the freedom of British society but it also suggests that British people with the right initiative and motivation could be equally successful. We, the Sikhs, are a proud people. All Sikh males adopt the name *Singh* meaning Lion and all females the name *Kaur* meaning Princess. Throughout our lives we remain lions and princessess. In Scotland your emblem is the lion rampant, symbol of a proud and dignified people. We too are lions in our own way and live and defend ourselves likewise.

Questions

1 How would you describe the writer of this piece of work? Support your observations with evidence from the passage.
2 What are your responses to the writer's observations about British people?
3 What seem to be the most important ways in which the Sikh culture is different to your own?
4 In what ways does John Singh experience racial prejudice, and how does he handle it?
5 What do you feel you have learned from reading John Singh's comments?
6 Are there any points raised in this article with which you disagree? Why?

My past life
Jagjeet Kaur

I am an Indian girl. I will tell you about my past life and my life since coming to England, and of what a critical time I had in the past and am having now.

I was born on 11 May 1956 in India. My parents were neither rich nor poor. I don't remember what happened when I was a child. I passed matriculation in six subjects with no problem. I did not go to college after school straight away because my father would not agree to higher education. He felt a girl's place was in the home, so education was a waste of money. Also if girls have higher education they will become modern and get out of the parents' control. I had always wanted to become a doctor and to prove that girls could do things the same as boys. I struggled for another two years and at last my father agreed and I went to college to study science subjects. Not for long though. Only four to five months later they arranged a marriage for me in England. So I had to leave my studies and get ready to come to England. I was not happy.

On 7 May 1977 I reached my in-law's house. It was like a hell. On 10 May I got married. Next day I was a house servant and slave. I didn't have any relations or friends in this country. I had to get up at six o'clock in the morning, cook breakfast for six children and send my husband to work. After this job, I had to brush the carpets of three rooms with a hand brush, wash all the dishes and clean the kitchen and front room before my mother and father-in-law woke up. When they got up I made tea and breakfast for them. When I finished that I had to wash the dishes again and start cooking food for the children for lunch. They had their lunch then I had to wash the dishes again. When I finished the work I had to wash my husband's clothes and the children's and clean the toilet. After finishing all the work it was four or five o'clock and the children came home from school. Then I had to give them something to eat and make tea for the whole lot. Then it was time to start cooking dinner for everyone. My husband used to go to a club so I had to wait to give him dinner about eleven or twelve o'clock. After all that I had to wash dishes and about one or half past one I used to go to bed. Next day it was the same.

I cried all the time but there was nobody who could help me. I didn't know anything about England so I couldn't think of going away somewhere because I was so scared. I couldn't send a letter to my parents because nobody gave me even a half-pence, never. One day I took some tablets and my husband took me to the hospital. I didn't want to live.

At the hospital I met an old Indian man who was from the same community as me. He made me his adopted daughter. He suggested I go back to my in-laws house because this is my religion. I went back and nobody spoke to me, not even my husband. It was worse than before. My mother-in-law was swearing a more lot at me.

My husband started beating me every day. My 'adopted father' came to see me three or four times but they said I was sleeping so he could not see me. My father-in-law said to 'father' that he should send me back to India or I would die. But my adopted father asked me not to go back. He asked me to call him and gave me his phone number if I needed help.

On 5 November 1977 (Guy Fawkes Day) they chucked me out of the house. It was raining outside. I did not have even a sweater on me. It was really cold. I went to the police station. My adopted father collected me and took me to his house. He had three daughters and two sons, all younger than me. I lived two years with them. I was working in a clothes factory in London then I moved to Bristol. I am now on a TOPS course and have met some nice people, but my first impressions of England were like a nightmare.

Questions

1 What was it about being an immigrant to this country that made the life of Jagjeet Kaur especially hard to bear?
2 In what ways did her husband and her in-laws mistreat her?
3 This piece reveals another side of arranged marriages. What would be the reasons behind this arrangement on a) her father's side, and b) her husband's?
4 What does this piece reveal about the differences between Western and Eastern attitudes towards women?
5 Did the fact that she was living in Britain help Jagjeet Kaur in any way; if so, how?
6 Can you suggest any ways in which this sort of disaster can be guarded against?

A morning bus ride
Rahul Barot

Rahul Barot came from Uganda in 1972, and his family settled down in Bristol. He studied at the University of Baroda, Gujarat State (India) for his BA in History and Hindi-English Literature. In Britain he did a teacher-training course in Cheltenham. He has worked as a teacher in Uganda and Guyana, and as a supply teacher in London; he has also worked as a labourer, a security guard and as a voluntary social worker. He has been writing in Gujarati, Hindi and English since the age of ten. Recently Rahul Barot won a literary award from South West Arts for a short story. He is now working for the Multi-Cultural Education Centre in Bristol.

The same Bristol green bus
Arrives at Shirehampton bus stop
It is number 28 and we all enter.
We don't push people to get in —
As people do in Bombay or Baroda —
But here people don't talk with each other,
Even when they meet every morning
For six months!
That does not happen in Delhi or Calcutta.

I show my Rover card and sit down.
Three Pakistani workers sitting opposite me
Have covered their tired faces
With their old anoraks.
One of them has kept his tiffin between his legs.
Everybody looking at them seems to say
'Poor little Asian workers! Pathetic! Pathetic!'
I wonder why these English people
Look at them in such a way.

They are certainly returning back
After their night shift,
Doing the dirty workers' jobs
No white men want to do.
The work has sucked all their energy.

Well, not all of it.
One man keeps talking in Punjabi
Which the English lady in the light coat
Does not understand:
I am sure if she understood,
She would have him turned off!

I smile at him, hoping
That in my smile he finds the Asiatic solidarity,
Divided though it is between
Hindus, Muslims, Buddhists, Sikhs,
And the Indian Christians —
Indian problems which generally
BBC 1 ignores and
ITV spares few moments for.

A young English lady enters.
One of the Pakistani men smiles eagerly at her —
Getting no response at all.
Another woman climbs onto the bus,
Wobbling past on high heels.
The Pakistani worker with the tiffin says,
'Ahy, why don't you sit with me, ah?'
He speaks in the Punjabi —
His erotic remarks in the early dawn
Produce no reaction whatever.

The bus stops on the Cheltenham Road.
Three exhausted Pakistani workers
Tumble onto the pavement.
Everybody looks at them from the window of the bus.
I smile at them.
They are running
Back home —
Leaving footprints on the bus stop
Which last only for a moment.

The alien
Pascale Petit

Lucienne looked at herself in the mirror. It was a three-piece folding mirror on the dressing-table. She cleaned the glass. Her profile was reflected from both sides. 'So, there are three of me,' she said, 'three more like me.' This thought consoled her. She picked up the bits of make-up strewn on the dressing-table — all blues and greens. 'Typically English' Lucienne thought to herself — 'Ugh!'

Her own olive complexion, black hair, and eyes, flashed back at her three times. The trouble was that she could never piece the three sides together — she had a friend who looked at her from the right, a friend who had only the front of a face, and another who owned only the left side.

'English people are three-dimensional' she realized. Lucienne resolved to become a better sculptor — she would create her own friends three-dimensionally. The trouble was that whenever people looked at her sculptures, her 'people', they tended to see them as aliens. This was probably due to the fact that they were glass-like, transparent, insubstantial. 'But that's all I know', Lucienne argued to herself. She left the dusting and hoovered the bedroom.

'This is the Master Bedroom.' Her prospective employer had told her. Lucienne had had trouble keeping a straight face. 'Presumably,' she thought, 'this is where the Master screwing goes on, to make the Master race.' Afterwards she shared the joke with her husband, who was Polish. They often criticised 'the English' together. It was a way of coming to terms with their own strangeness. It was the link that brought them both together.

'Of course, if I lived in France,' she sighed, 'I wouldn't be classed as a cleaner, and therefore the lowest of the low, but as an artist and intellectual — I only clean so I can be as creative as possible for as much of my time as possible.' But the English were rigidly class-conscious. Actually, she was very confused, not sure which class she belonged to — since she must belong to one — and not be different, as she was.

The most offensive thing about this country had struck her as soon as she arrived, as a child — the food. She had accused her grandmother of poisoning her. Twenty years on, she could still remember, with nostalgia, the taste of real ham, real mince, real French food. And then there was this complete lack of dress-sense, and visual flair, hence the awful eyeshadows scattered on the dressing-table. English women had no idea how to look good. However they had the advantage over French girls of being naturally healthy-looking.

Lucienne turned away from the mirror which had once again magnetized her. Who was she? She stared down at her body. It was an odd view, from the top, and not as others saw her. Of course, she was abnormally vain — but really her obsession came more from a need to know why and how she was so different. Even in France she would have been frowned upon, being a Pied Noir. Her father's side of the family came from Algeria.

Once, she had tried to conform by being self-employed. She had learnt how to make hats, but ended up creating exotic Arabian fantasies for rich foreign royalty. Where did this exotic streak originate from? At the time she had been ignorant of her father's Algerian connections. An aunt had informed her of this. But her mother had denied it. Who was she to believe? Then Joan had gone to France on holiday and seen a book called 'Les Femmes Algériennes,' had returned and told Lucienne: 'If I had had the money I would have bought it for you — it's proof — their features were just like yours when you're deeply tanned — including your funny nose.' Lucienne wished she could have seen the evidence for herself.

Meanwhile, she continued to live in England, as invisibly as she could. Her job as a cleaner made her invisible. She had only to enter a room, and people would keep on chatting, as if she was not there, looking through her, as if she were transparent. At lunchtime she was discreetly hidden in the back kitchen, to eat quietly staring out of the window. Friends of the children would ask 'Who was that?' and an eighteen-year old son might answer 'Oh, just the cleaning-lady.' This suited Lucienne. She did not belong so she wanted to join her glass friends in the mirror. She lost weight purposely from overwork — both on her sculptures, and from cleaning. She grew thin, and disguised her small body with bulky English clothes, such as jeans and legwarmers. She could not vote, and was secretly relieved not to have to — the politics of this country worried her.

Her one ambition was to transmute her form through art, to make new manifestations of herself through her imagination. She spun threads of glass from her eyes towards mirrors. Her glass friends became more ornate, more real, in fact, than herself. She was only really happy when talking to them. They answered her in ways she understood. 'Other women have children' she thought, 'but my body isn't real enough for such a physical act such as child-bearing. Could a baby grow inside me? No.' She turned to her sculptures for consolation, and made glass foetuses inside their wombs. She imagined their lovers making love to them so that they climaxed in a moment of melding, as the Cabbala had described — as, indeed, many people described. Lucienne couldn't imagine two people joining. 'It must happen to other people — that's why they're not as lonely as me.' She decided.

Her mother had been made of glass. When she had given birth to Lucienne, she had cracked, and gone mad. 'That would happen to me' Lucienne knew.

There were many disadvantages to being made of glass. 'I have no protection from light and sound, no opaque covering of flesh to protect me.' Her sculptures looked back at her. Lucienne had made one of them a glass brain, the nerve-endings exposed to every little draught, which it must feel, as a person undergoing plastic surgery. Lucienne wanted very much to scream, but she had no voice. Being an alien was difficult. Instead she cried. The tears gathered in pools at her feet and vitrified.

Questions

1 What blanket criticisms does the character in this story make of the English? Would you accept them as being fair comment? What response would you make to these criticisms?

2 In what way does the title of this story help you to understand it?

3 What aspects of this story suggest that the narrator is going mad, and why do you think this is happening to her?

4 How does the narrator's family background contribute to her feeling of being an 'outsider'?

5 What is your response to this story? Did you like it; hate it; not understand it? What purpose do you think the author had in writing it?

Britain through Arab spectacles

Nada Zeineddine

*Nada Zeineddine is 32 and comes from Syria. The early part of her
childhood was spent accompanying her parents on several trips abroad, but
with the exception of three years schooling in Cairo, she received her
education in Syria. At the University of Damascus she studied for a BA in
English Literature and she first came to England in 1976 to study for her MA
in English and American Literature at the University of Leicester. She
returned to England for 1980 – 1984 to work on her PhD thesis on the
problems of identity faced by women and artists in the plays of Ibsen, Miller
and Williams. She is now a lecturer at Damascus University specialising in
drama.*

*Nada Zeineddine is presently working on a study of Ibsen in the Arab
world, a translation of Ibsen's letters into Arabic, and a comparative study of
Ibsen and Miller in English.*

A few raindrops on the window-pane told me we must be circling over
the British Isles, and the clouds heavily veiling what lay below were
sufficient indications to a weary traveller like myself that this was the
address I had jotted down in my mind for a few years — England. As the
plane plunged into the clouds, and finally bumped onto the runway, I
suddenly felt courageous enough to abandon my childish thoughts of
being a stowaway on the return flight home.

Syrian Arab Airlines had faithfully deposited my baggage, my fears
and hopes, and myself on a Heathrow patch.

Picking my way through the mazes and mazes of corridors, I was
struck by the relative quietness of it all. The only indignant voice came
from some American in the queue, who felt that the pace at which the
queue was moving was snail-like and that had this been
American — 'Jesus, we would have landed on the moon by now.' I could
not help but be amused — things were starting to draw me out of my
cloudy frame of mind.

It was done. There I was — on the other side of the Immigration
Officer. My passport duly stamped, the course of English and American
studies which I had come to pursue carefully jotted down. The Syrian
carrier was no longer visible to me. Trolleys of luggage swirled around

me. Red double-decker coaches consumed people on the pavement. I, soon found myself staring out of the window of a coach at a sign reading 'Arrivals'. 'My God, where is the "Departure" sign?' thought I. But new impressions soon jostled in my mind. As the wheels rolled along on the wrong side of the road, I soon drifted away from home and into a new realm of experience.

Naturally, the coach was full of people of various nationalities — Brits returning from their summer holidays boasting their 'exported' sun-tans; Americans pocketing their lives' savings to see Shakespeare-land; Pakistanis rejoining their families in England — and bewildered students like myself.

I was dragged out of myself by a voice: 'Is this your first trip to England, love?'

My hackles were raised. How dare the man call me 'love'? Surely, he should have more respect for the whiteness of his hair, and more respect for a woman he does not know? That man is dangerous, said the voice of my upbringing. I had been brought up to believe that any approach from a man — verbal or otherwise, must be shunned and distrusted.

A bunch of American girls nearly jumped out of the window when the coach rounded a corner in London. The cause of this sudden commotion was the appearance of what they referred to as 'Haaarods'. I could not recall a museum by that name in my guide-book and I got even more confused when one of the girls announced to her chums that they could come shopping here tomorrow. I did not know that things in a museum were for sale, or that the majestic buildings of London were often a collaboration between history and commerce.

So it started. And in the course of my life in England I came up again and again against this blend of cultures, this meeting and melting, or meeting and clashing. Again and again, I found myself thinking of Rudyard Kipling's famous line, 'Never the twain shall meet'. I was rather puzzled — why was he so adamant about the fact that his twain, east and west, would remain separate. Is it already decided, or does every individual living abroad have·to decide on its finality?

I had come to study for a higher degree in English and American literature, and it was this that acted as a basis for nearly all my experiences. Life in a British University offered a contrast to life as an undergraduate at home. To sit down in a group not exceeding ten or twelve people and freely discuss various angles of work from various viewpoints was, for me, a sheer luxury and a splitting headache. It was nice to be in a tiny group compared to the huge numbers admitted into universities at home. However, the group was highly selected, and much to my dismay I found that certain areas of the experience of literature were blocked to my understanding. In the course of my discussions with my colleagues, I found myself again and again being puzzled by attitudes towards religion and towards God. Brought up in the Islamic faith, I could not but stiffen over any debate as to whether God was dead or alive, whether he had fathered a son or not. I could not be objective. By contrast, my colleagues had the gift of objectivity, and could see the issue as separate from themselves. They had more tolerance, were more detached. I have come to believe in the benefits of detachment, which is not to say that I could or can always achieve a measure of it. Like everyone, I suppose, I had my vulnerable spots and these were invariably related to religion and politics.

In contrast to this academic world, with its cold moments and frustrations, people in general outside the university offered an even more varied and sometimes more interesting way of seeing life. I was fortunate or unfortunate to live in a Young Women's Christian Association hostel. Not only did that place bring me up against contradictions denoted by the discrepancy between the name of the hostel and my Muslim faith, but introduced an elastic concept of 'youth', housing women of all ages and many different types of background. But on the other hand this elasticity and variety were not without their rewards and punishments. The YWCA was like a bee hive in which a queen appeared every once in a while, buzzing its way into everyone else's lives. A member of the older generation would preside over the affairs of this female kingdom. With a mixture of curiousity and malice it would touch on every resident's life, drawing the juice of human experience and injecting bits and pieces of advice where needed. This busy bee attitude, at which some of the residents were experts, irked me and caused me no end of aggravation. The building constituted rows and rows of rooms. What the residents shared in common was a set of kitchens: the downstairs kitchen and the upstairs one. Your belonging to one kitchen or another was destined by the choice of a locker and a 'cell' number. As it happened, I was allocated to the underworld camp. In the downstairs kitchen, round the stoves and grills, clustered women of wide-ranging interests or disinterests, students and non-students, each with a background of experiences so alien to the other that conversation often had to be restricted to the most common of experiences — eating and drinking. Occasionally the place would sparkle with talk of unemployment, family rifts and so on — experiences that would be labouring so much in somebody's soul that the need for listeners broke the barriers of apathy which very often separated us. Advice was dished out by the queen of the hive — a lady who had 'A Lover' and was waiting for his return behind a YWCA wall. Every day she would have breakfast, looking immaculate with curlers ready to pop out of her head the minute Alan, who had disappeared three years ago, popped up again. The disappearance was hardly surprising. Now whether there had ever been an Alan I never really got to know. All I know is that frustration seemed to be a keynote to many and became in itself a vicious circle breeding other vicious circles. In the course of my stay in England, I learnt that the family structure was quite alien to anything I had known. While I waited impatiently for a letter from home to bless my otherwise forlorn pigeonhole, another resident was only allowed to go home on Sunday, and even then her mother made her pay for her tea and biscuits! That is of course an extreme case of neurotic behaviour on the part of the mother. It did, however, serve to highlight for me the need to realize that while the sanction of family relations was indispensible, it was very often, as in my case, hampering because it never ceased to pull you back when you needed to move forward. Somehow self-fulfilment for me became tinged with feelings of guilt and disloyalty towards the family. While the case of the resident was to me cruel and equally stunting, it represented to me the other side of the coin, the side my culture would never consciously flip. At the cost of hypocrisy, hatred and bitter rows, families in Syna stick together — often across generations. You only leave your family for some convincing reason like marriage — particularly, of course, if you have the misfortune of having been born female.

Oh, that was a raw spot for me — my womanhood — and still is. It is continually thrown into your face as though you have to bear the burden of what was purely nature's choice and its way of propogating the human race. But in my country, somehow, the meaning of propogation is unstable as a woman represents a minus not a plus. My English friends had launched out on their own at the age of eighteen and could now enjoy the freedom of their choices and the privilege of privacy. I had been made to seek a place like the YWCA, to remain in a women's exclusive citadel, almost as if the invilgilating warden could lock away any indiscretions and curb any needs for freedom, so that you were transferred from one home setting to another, from one jailor to another. That one could be one's own jailor, or one's own self-imposed prisoner, never occurred to me then. In fact, I did not even see it as an insult to my individuality. All I know is that I willingly trudged along the path of conformity. It was too deeply ingrained in me to alter. In fact, I felt secure and snug in these restrictive impositions.

It was not only my inherited attitudes towards myself that made womanhood a pain in the neck. It was also the inherited attitudes of the English towards me. I was regarded with a mixture of amusement and suspicion. There was something about a woman leaving home for a stack of books on literature that might, in all probability, end up on a kitchen shelf, that was unconvincing. I was an avant-garde Muslim, an Arab woman spreading her wings for the duration of a course of studies only to return to the safety net of her purdah. This attitude towards a somewhat mistaken identity irritated me — not only because it was not built on any firm foundation, but also because it served to make me aware of the limited view of the English towards the Arabs. Nearly everyone I came across gaped with astonishment when I said I had come from the Middle East. To start with, Syria, Turkey and Iran seemed to have no boundaries — geographical, linguistic or otherwise. Furthermore, the image of an Arab is that of a grizzly bear wrapped in yards of black cloth, possessing a few oil wells, a fat bank account, a camel and with any number (out of four) wives to one man. While those conceptions are not entirely wrong, the English are often only too prepared to think of the Arab world as homogenous. While some Arab countries and some sections within Arab countries do live a type of 'One Thousand and One Nights' existence, others have been forced into major social upheavals — but no, it was all the same to the English, Arabs inhabited a world of sheep and dairy products. It would be unfair to exempt the Arab world or members of it from responsibility for this image, but it is also the way of the world to believe what it wants to believe. What the English have beneficially done for me through their atitudes is teach me to laugh at myself and my culture — not with the mocking savagery of criticism directed towards myself and others, but with bemused scepticism of Arab notions of themselves, and of the English of themselves.

Anyone leaving their country for any length of time stands the risk of being blessed or condemned by this position of standing on the fringe of his or her own society and of that of the host country. I have often admired the quality that the English have for standing on the fringe of their experience while being in their own homeland. They laugh at themselves, their politicians, their habits, and history — at nearly everything under their elusive sun. Underneath the bubbles of critical laughter lies a pride — powerful and pervasive — a national pride and a staunch loyalty I never cease to find admirable. While being able to stand outside themselves, the English can when needs arise retreat into the privacy of their own lives which they guard fiercely. What I found incomprehensible is the fact that very often the need for privacy could shut out elderly members of the family who would then be safely conducted to old people's homes, a form of social welfare not available in my country because families stick together through hell or high water, which very often includes senile, ageing parents, grandparents, aunts and so on. I recall a particular old lady I used to see every morning. In fact, her spaniels and herself soon became part of my daily routine. Having left the introductions to the spaniels, it took us a few weeks to start nodding to each other. Finally the silence was broken one morning when the lady asked me whether today was Sunday or Wednesday? She had got the two poles of the week alright but it happened to be Friday. Anyway, it transpired that her 'telly' had broken down and somehow she had lost touch with time. She sounded like a character out of a Beckett play touching at some void. But loneliness, through choice or necessity, was a problem. In an Arab country you can easily be saddled by the elderly, so much so that your privacy as a younger family member becomes almost non-existent. The boundaries of your own home and life are forced into being flexible enough to admit others who impinge on you sometimes lovingly and sometimes parasitically.

In daily life, and in my university life, the English language never ceased to taunt me with irregularities and fascinating idioms which had started to haunt me ever since that man called me 'love'. Words seemed to bear no relation to what they said. I had been taught a set of idioms, memorised them, without quite knowing how to use them or indeed why they were being used. I still cannot figure out how it came to be raining 'cats and dogs', or how you 'burn your boats' when you are miles away from the sea. This is not to deny the power of any figurative language, rather it is to indicate that idiomatic usage, to me, was a typical British experience of the language and that you had to 'pick your own' understanding of them as you went along. I suffered many embarrassments over my own misunderstanding of language. I was once told that I looked 'under the weather' and that I did not seem quite 'with it'. I nearly looked around me for that mysterious 'it', but could not for the life of me paraphrase that 'under the weather' business. Small wonder that I could not — what with the swirling clouds of new experiences, I was bound to look drawn and lost. But the funny bit about it is the underlying assumption that the weather should be bad. The weather, in fact, both in conversation and experience was an endless source of fascination to me. As a daily topic it served to break silences between strangers, to ward off more personal expressions between acquaintances, and last but not least, to comment on a freak of nature that plagued this island sometimes but touched it with a magic wand at others. It was almost too illogical for any explanation, and too unpredictable to act as a background to a nation that, I would safely say, is on the predictable side. The weather turned my umbrella into my best and most loyal friend.

'Come on', I say to myself, 'be fair'. I cannot help but be moved as I look back on my experiences by the ways the English respond to your needs when they are urgent. I naturally lived through some bad patches but did not live through them alone. People went out of their way to offer advice and understanding, so much so that my own understanding of the term 'home' gradually underwent a change. You are made to feel at home, and can slowly build a home based on columns that are not necessarily inherited, but that you can make for yourself once given the groundwork. To share life's experiences out of sincerity, not because you are a permanent fixture in a place, or happen to be someone's daughter or sister, afforded for me a measure of security which I came to enjoy. There is no need to live an extroverted life just because that is held to be the ideal, and the expected. The knowledge that you are not taken for granted is precious.

It was very interesting to meet people from other cultures who offered a comparative line of judgment for my experiences. It was also a test as to how I rated the English. There were a few occasions when I 'ganged up' with other foreigners in my criticism against English ways of life, but others when I only discovered how much I loved the English through my feelings of outraged indignation over what I held to be disgruntled and self-complacent remarks coming from foreigners. I met an Italian who measured the soundness of English values by the absence of pastas from an English menu. 'In Ittttaly', she said, 'people looked after their stomachs but in England people don't know how to eatt'. Fish and chips and Yorkshire Pudding on the menu were, to her, a source of affliction — a daily reminder of all that England could never aspire to be.

Among the elderly, I have found a general disapproval of the ways in which foreigners came to live in England. The younger generation seemed more tolerant. I can remember two incidents in which prejudice became clearly expressed. They both took place on British Rail. The guard once announced that we were approaching St Pancras Station. His flavoured accent was unmistakably Indian. My neighbours in the compartment looked around and exclaimed, 'Well, well, well, I jolly well hope that this is London's St Pancras, not Bombay's. On another occasion, I saw a lady visibly shrivel up in the far corner of her window seat, and struggle with her best manners when a Pakistani family joined the train and one of the children literally clambered over her in the act of wanting to stare out of the window. I thought she was dying of horror and a prejudiced heart. I suppose tolerance and intolerance rule every nation but the general consensus among the elderly that if the English Channel froze over one winter the world would be cut off from England, is painful.

During my sojourn here I kept wishing that the English would make an attempt at transposing themselves into other cultures and languages. But it is often, I kept reminding myself, the language that is responsible for this cultural insularity. The average British citizen I found is well-informed; the media covers the many-sidedness of a situation, and the English language being international, there is no need for the English to learn anything else. As for what happens outside England, well very often compassion is expressed, but that is about it. But then, am I not expecting too much? We are funny creatures, seeing the fault and perpetrating it, making allowances and criticism in one breath.

England to me has been so much more than a place. It is my experience of a certain place, and a certain people — an experience that has threatened to disinherit me of what would or allegedly should be my own experience. I shall, in all probability, go back to hear my own voice and my own experience separating me from many values, beliefs and attitudes that I had previously taken for granted. 'England, your England', my fellow countrymen will chime chorically. But enduring the separateness is well worth it. Syrian Arab Airlines would want to reclaim me in exactly the same dimensions in which it has deposited me. I may be smaller or bigger than the slot I left behind. But maybe if I am no longer willing to fit into it, I may help to make room for myself and possibly for others. Who knows, the result may be sheer misery or sheer bliss? It is, though, a cause worth championing.

I can see my homeland beckoning to me. I can imagine the arms stretching out to embrace me, the welcoming faces lighting up to greet me. How different they all look, I shall think. Or are my eyes any different? I will no doubt return the embraces, the smiles, and will in turn embrace some loved values I have been missing. But in my heart there will be a yearning for a homeland that is not mine, yet is exclusively mine. I do not think I can leave it behind. It is too meaningful an extension of myself, at least to me. It will be in me somewhere — distant yet distinctly near. The sun will be beating down on the Damascus runway. Do I translate it into sunshine or a veil of clouds?? (Oh that painfully typical British habit I have acquired; the weather hiding foreseeable nostalgia, in one puff of a breath, in one sight.) Only time may unfold the answer.

Questions

1 What kind of differences does the narrator find between her own culture and the one she finds in Britain?
2 What does the narrator seem to have learned through the experience of living in another culture?
3 What does the narrator like about the English? Do you think her observations apply to all British people?

Sonny's lettah (anti-sus poem)
Linton Kwesi Johnson

Brixton Prison,
Jebb Avenue,
London SW2,
England.

Dear Mama,
Good Day.
I hope dat wen
deze few lines reach y'u,
they may find y'u in di bes' af helt.

Mama,
I really doan know how fi tell y'u dis,
cause I did mek a salim pramis
fi tek care a lickle Jim
an' try mi bes' fi look out fi him.

Mama,
Ah really did try mi bes',
but none-di-les',
mis sarry fi tell y'u seh
poor lickle Jim get arres'.

It woz di miggle a di rush howah
wen everybady jus' a hus'le an' a bus'le
fi goh home fi dem evenin' showah;
mi an' Jim stan-up
waitin' pan a bus,
nat causin' no fus',
wen all an a sudden
a police van pull-up.

Out jump t'ree policeman,
di 'hole a dem carryin' batan.
Dem waak straight up to mi an' Jim.
One a dem hol' an to Jim
seh him tekin him in;
Jim tell him fi let goh a him
far him noh dhu not'n',

an him naw t'ief,
nat even a but'n.
Jim start to wriggle.
Di police start to giggle.

Mama,
mek Ah tell y'u whey dem dhu to Jim;
Mama,
mek Ah tell y'u whey dem dhu to him:

dem t'ump him in him belly
an' it turn to jelly
dem lick him pan him back
an' him rib get pap
dem lick him pan him he'd
but it tuff like le'd
dem kick him in him seed
an' it started to bleed

Mama,
Ah jus' could'n' stan-up deh
an' noh dhu not'n':
soh mi jook one in him eye
an' him started to cry;
mi t'ump one in him mout'
an' him started to shout
mi kick one pan him shin
an' him started to spin
mi t'ump him pan him chin
an' him drap pan a bin

an' crash
an de'd.

Mama,
more policeman come dung
an' beat me to di grung;
dem charge Jim fi sus;
dem charge mi fi murdah.

Mama,
doan fret,
doan get depres'
an' doun-hearted
Be af good courage
till I hear fram you.

I remain,
your son,
Sonny.

Questions

1 What does this poem gain being written in the rhythms and forms of natural West Indian speech?
2 Describe in your own words the event that the poem recounts.
3 What are your feelings about this poem? Does it exaggerate anything, or does it seem true to life? Do you blame Sonny for anything that happened?

Nice – a monologue
Mustapha Matura

Mustapha Matura was born in Trinidad; he came to England in 1960. His first full length play As time goes by *won him both the George Devine and John Whiting Awards in 1971, and was mounted by the Traverse Theatre, Edinburgh followed by the Royal Court in London.*

Bakerloo line (1972) and the monologue Nice *(1973) were both staged by the Almost Free Theatre.* Nice *is frequently performed; it was staged at the Arena Stage, Washington in 1980.* Rum 'n coca cola *was produced at the Royal Court in 1976 and at the Brooklyn Academy New York in the same year.*

In 1978 he founded the Black Theatre Co-Operative with director Charlie Hanson to encourage West Indian playwrights and actors.

His first television work was the joint project entitled No problem *between the Black Theatre Co-Operative and London Weekend Television with Channel 4. The series proved a great success; the third series has recently been shown.*

Mustapha continues to write for stage, but is now very involved in the writing and development of Black silk, *a new drama series for BBC TV.*

Many of his plays are published in this country and in the USA.

Scene: *a prison canteen (tables and chairs); in it a black man in uniform is wiping and sweeping. He speaks directly to audience.*

Man: Wen a come off de boat de customs man was nice ter me, so I was nice back ter him, but a friend a mine who come ter meet me say, boy yer should'nt be nice ter dem, dey do like we, but I say nar man it en so, it en so at all, wen people nice ter you, you must be nice back ter dem, an if yer want people ter be nice ter you, you must be nice ter dem, but anyhow he say a was foolish an a go fine out, but a was nice ter he so de next day he carry me down ter de exchange dey call it, an de man dey was nice ter me too, so a was nice back ter him, so wen dey give me dis job sweeping out a office, I say tank you ter de man, an he say tank you back ter me,

but me friend say, a should'nt say tank you ter him, but I say de man say tank you ter me so I say tank you back ter him, an I tell him if yer want people ter say tank you ter you you have ter say tank you ter dem, but he say how a was wrong, but I say nar man, I en wrong I rite, den he say how I stupid, but anyhow a say tank you ter him, so de next night he carry me ter a night club, wher dey had some girls dancing wit coloured men, de first time a see white woman dance wit coloured man, an dey en dancing straight an back yer no, dey dancing wit dey bottom all over de place, so I say boy dis is de place fer me, so a went up an ask one a de girls nice fer a dance an she dance wit me an it was a good dance an we had a good time. But me friend pull me aside an say boy, how a go teach yer ter live in dis country wen yer do listen ter me, yer must'nt be nice ter dem, dey do want yer ter be nice ter dem, but I say nar man, dat en true because I was nice ter she an she was nice back ter me, but he say de same ting again dat I go fine out, so a miss a dance trying ter fine out, but a en find out notting, so a went back an ask she ter dance an she say yes an we dance again, but a notice me friend was'nt dancing at all, so a say he must be en feel like dancing or maybe he foot hurting him, so anyhow wen de club start ter close me friend come pulling me saying le we go, le we go, but I say nar man, I go ask de lady ter go home wit she an see wha she say, but me friend say dey do want we in dey house much less in dey bed, he say dey only like ter dance wit we an get hot ter go an heat up de white boys, but I say nar man, dat en true, because I no dat if you heat up someting is you have ter eat it but he say I en no dese woman an I en go get notting off she an dat if a go wit she, in de morning she go cry out an say a hypnotise she an rape she, but I say nar man, it en so if a woman heat you up she heat you up fer a reason, an de reason is because she want you terburn she, but he say I is a idiot an a go fine out but anyhow a ask she nicely ter come home wit she an she say yes, so a leave me friend outside de club, an me an she went home an had a nice time an in de morning she en cry out an bawl rape or anyting she just say she have ter go ter work an if a does go ter de club often, she go see me again, so I say yes a does go sometimes an a hope a go see she again, an she say she hope so too, so a went outside an a didn't even no where a was but a ask a police man nice an he tell me how ter catch a bus back ter me friends house, boy wen a tell me friend wha happen yer shoulda see de man, de man went mad, de man start ter cuss me an call me all kinda names an tell me a shouldn't ask no policeman notting dat if yer ask dem anyting an dey fine out yer new dey go lock yer up fer someting, but I say nar man, if yer want ter fine out anyting is a policeman ter ask an if yer ask dem nice dey go answer yer back nice but he say a go fine out, but I say how a go fine out he just say a go fine out, but anyhow a was nice ter him so he take me ter de pub wit him, so wen we get inside de pub, I say le me buy de drinks, he say no, a must'nt buy drinks fer people, a must le dem buy de own drinks if a buy drinks fer dem dey go tink a stupid an drink up all me money, but I say nar man, it en so, if yer buy people drink dey go buy yer back a drink, but he say de same ting again how a foolish an how a go fine out, an if a don't hear a go feel, so anyhow dey had a white man stanning up next ter me so a buy him a drink an he buy he back a drink, so a say well if he buy me back drink, a have ter buy me back drink an so it go on until me friend say yer see wha a tell yer de man go drink out all yer money but I say nar man, dat en go happen, but anyhow he say he going next door ter de betting shop an wen a ready ter go come fer him, so wen time come fer de pub ter close de white man a tink he name was Fred, Fred tell me he have a bet ter put on, dat he get some tip from some horses mouth an if a have any money ter put it on it, so we went next door an put on de bet, a notice me friend wasn't looking too happy, so a say wha wrong man, he say he lost all he money, so I say well, look de man just give me a tip an he say ter put all yer money on it, but he say dey en go give no coloured man horse ter back on, because dey en want ter see no coloured man win money, so I say nar man, because he just put he own money on it, but he say da is a trick ter fool me, but I say he fool he self because he put more money dan me, anyhow de horse come twenty ter one so I en do bad at all anyhow a give me friend a five pound note an we went home wen we get dey who could be waiting fer we but de girl from de club, de same girl a meet last night, she say how she pass in ter see if a was going ter de club later, a musta tell she where a was living, but I say well if yer going ter de club ter night yer might as well stay here an wen time come fer we ter go we could go together so she come inside an me friend say dat if people see she come after work dey go say dat she working fer me, but I say nar man, dey car say dat, I only meet she last night how dey go say dat, but he say a go fine out an dat he going an see a film round de corner, now dat surprise me because I no he was'nt no theatre man, but a say he must be feeling lonely so anyhow de girl take off she shoes an start ter clean up de place, an wen she done she say wha we have ter eat, I tell she notting, she say not ter worry dat she go go round de corner an get sone ting, so I say da is awright wit me, so she went, wen she come back de woman cook one food, pardner a never no white woman could cook so, so a say wat dis woman is someting boy, an den after we finish eat she take off all she clothes an say she want de same dat a give she last night, so I say awright an give she it an we had a nice time man, wen time come fer we ter go ter de club, she say she tired so I say well le we stay here so she say right is alright wit she, so da is how we spend de night, I en even no wat time me friend come in, wen he come in I en even hear im a just feel im trying ter pull de girl in he half a de bed, but she musta be too heavy fer he, because he give up quick, but in de mornng a went ter work an leave she dey wit him so I en wha happen wen a come back home de night an tell de man wat a nice foreman a had yer shoulda see de man go mad, just like wid de policeman so ter change de subject, a ask him wha bout de girl if she get out awright he say yes but a shouldn't tink de foreman nice because dey en nice an dat he job is ter make coloured people work hard, but I say nar man, dat en true dem have ter work hard too, but he say is a different kinda work, but I say work is work an if yer working someplace wit people yer have ter be nice wit dem, but he say how a go learn, an how de girl leave a message saying how she go be at de club ter night an dat I must come, so a tell im tank yer, but boy a was feeling so tired I say I en going ter noo club ternight he say, yer see how tired yer is, is because de foreman working yer hard, but I no a was tired fer someting else, but he say it was de foreman so I en say notting, anyhow bout twelve a clock de door bell start ter ring, who it could be but de girl, de same girl from de club, de girl who come home here an cook me a meal, she say she en see me in de club an she come ter see if anyting wrong wit me, but I say nar man, nottin en wrong I just taking a rest da is all, so a ask she if she want ter come in an stay, but she an me friend say de same ting, she say she en want ter stay, an me friend say he en want she ter stay, so a figure dey musta have a row or someting anyhow a put on me clothes an went round by she an we had a good time again, wen a come back from work dat night, me friend say boy, wha yer doing de woman go kill yer, I say nar man, she en go kill, me, den he say dem white woman could take more man dan we no, so den I ask him how he go feel, if a move out because is me an he was paying de rent? Well boy de man went mad again, just like wit de policeman, an wit de foreman, he start ter cuss me an say how a ungrateful, an how is he who look after me wen a first come ter dis country, an is my people beg him ter look out ter fer me, an how now I want ter left him in a lurch, boy a never see a man go so crazy, an den he ask me if a moving in wit de girl, so I tell im a wasn't sure as yet but a was tinking of it, well is den he start ter cuss me, an buse me, well boy wha a could do, but say tank yer fer looking after me but I en want yer ter look after me no more, an a go pack up and leave by ter night, but yer see deep down inside I no he was a nice guy, because he en charge me no rent fer de four days a stay by he, any how a move in wit dis girl, well it was awright wen we first start, but den de woman start ter do all kinda a ting like tell me how a mustn't wear sock in bed, I tell she a cole, an how a mustn't wear me pajamas under me clothes, again a tell she it cole, but it like she en hear an how I mustn't be nice ter de woman next door, an one set a I must do dis an I mustn't do dis, so I tell she nar man, dat en go happen because fer one ting wen it a cole me en want ter take of no pajamas is den yer go catch cole, but she en listen, she tell me I stupid an I en no bout dis country, an dat de woman next door go believe I after someting because I so nice ter her, but I tell she nar man it en so, is wen yer nice ter people dey go be nice ter you, but den she come like me friend she call me idiot an burke a was going an tell she me name wasn't Burke but a was too tired, so anyhow one day wen a come home from work, just as a reach de top a de stairs, who should come outa she door but de woman from next door, so I give she a howdy like a does do anytime a does see she, anyhow dis time she ask me if a have a shilling fer de meter, well a tell she I en have no shilling on me but a have one inside on de mantlepiece, she say go in fer it, so I say awright, an a open door, soon as de woman come in de room, de woman start ter get on, de woman start ter tell me all kinda ting like how I so nice an she like me because I so nice, so I tell she I tink she nice too, an yer no de wat next ting a no is me an de woman having a nice time on de bed, den de woman start ter bawl an groan like she never want ter stop, so me en stop she, de next ting a no is de door bust open an who should come in but, de girl who a living wit, de same girl from de club, well boy a never jump so fast, but it en me she go fer as de woman next door, both a dem start ter cuss one another an row a never no white woman could cuss so much, de girl tell de woman how she is a hoe, an de woman tell de girl how she is a slut, an how she wouldn't push me wit a barge pole, an how is me who pull she in de room an give she a asprin an take advantage a she headache, so boy yer could imagine de fix a in, so right dere an den a say de best ting ter do is go, so whilst both a dem rowing a pick up me bag an put me clothes in it, an as a hit de door, de girl turn round an notice a going, she say wha yer going, a say a going an stay wit me friend, boy de girl start ter cry an break down an tell me all kinda ting like how she love me an she car live witout me an how if a left she go kill she self, well boy dat slow me down, but is wen she tell me she go do anyting fer me den a stop, well by den de woman from next door gone, after a tell she tank you fer coming in, an she tell me tanks fer de shilling, so den de girl tell me how she go look after me an make sure I en have ter work because she no I en like ter go ter work in de cole, well she was right dey, an another ting is she say she go bring enough money fer both a we, well boy wha a could say ter dat, a tell she tanks dat da is alright wit me, an she say alright too as long as a do leave, well a put down me bag an is den she start ter tell me how she love me an how no man ever please she like how I please she, so anyhow tings start ter go good a went in an tell de foreman tank you fer de job an how a go be leaving soon an he say well how he go miss me an how it was nice having me work fer him, an ting, so pardner tings start ter get good de girl start ter work so hard dat after a while a never get ter see she, she go out ter work an wen she come back she sleep, but I didn't mind so much because everytime she come in she used ter bring in one set a five pound notes a never see so much money in me life, boy a tell yer I'd go out side an spend an spend an de money still wouldn't done, so after awhile a start ter save it, anyhow a didn't mind not seeing she so much because de woman from next door used ter cook me food an bring it in an me an she use ter have a good time, so a couldn't complain too much, now de next ting a no is she too say she want ter go out an work fer me because she could do better dan de girl, an how she have more contacts an she could work harder, so I say awright den give it a try no harm in trying an see if yer like it, so anyhow she look happy wen a tell she dat, but de only ting was worrying me is who go cook me food, because wit both a dem out a go starve, but anyhow a say well if tings turn out so wha a go do, but as soon as a say dat wat should happen but a knock on de door, an who it could be but de landlady she say she come ter collect some rent, so I tell she ter hold on a minute an le me open de door well she come in de room ter collect some rent but I feel she come in ter look around, so I en say notting because is she place an if she want ter look around an see wha going she have a right ter do dat, anyhow we sit down talking an de next ting a no is how she start ter tell me bout she husband an how bad he does treat she an how he do give she notting so I say well some man like dat an she say how I nice an how I understand an how she feel she could talk ter me, so I say tank you because if people feel dey could talk ter you dey must be like you, so boy we sit down dey talking, all morning an den she say well is lunch time an she have ter go down an cook an how nice it was talking ter me an she sorry how she take up all me time, but I tell she nar man, it en so is awright I enjoy it so den she say eow she go make up fer it by bringing some lunch fer me so I say awright den if da is wat yer want ter do, do nottin else, so anyhow she bring up de lunch and a must say she cooking was'nt so hot but I tell she it taste nice an she like dat because de next ting she do is ter give me a hug an a kiss, so I say well if yer want ter give me a hug an kiss, I want ter give you a hug an kiss too, well she say she would like dat because is a long time no man hug she an kiss she, not because no man en want ter do it but because she en want any kinda man ter do it, de man she want ter do it must be a nice man, an he must be a kind man an he must understand she well I tell she she right ter want dat anyhow me an she had a good time man, everyday she used ter cook me food an come up an me an she would have a good time until she husband come home from work den a wouldn't see she but a would no she was dey because sometimes she would start singing, I love you baby, an I need you baby, an sometimes she would collect de rent in de morning an put it back under de door in de evening, so I no she was dere, anyhow one day me an she husband was talking an he say how dat he always wanted ter go ter de West Indies because de people always so happy an nice so I tell im dat if he tink de people so nice over here he should go down dere an he go see how nice dey really is an I even tell him how if he go down dere he could stay wit my people an dem an he say how nice dat was an tank me an ting, so after dat me an he was de best a friend an he used ter ask me tings like he hope he wife singing do bodder me an I no how woman was, I say nar man, I do mind I like she singing an I glad ter hear people singing, because wen dey do dat it mean dey happy, an I like ter no people happy, an is a funny ting because den he used ter get serious but den he would start smiling again, so he was alright an yer no someting he never used ter take me ter he pub but everytime he come back he used ter bring me a guiness, yer could beat dat everytime like de sun rise, but a never fine out wha he used ter mean by do kill meself guiness car kill, but anyhow he was me mate, de first mate a ever had, anyhow yer see how some people could be nice, so one day a buy one a dem Jaguar cars an who a should see crossing de road in front a me, right cross me bonnet but me friend, me same friend who meet me off de boat, so I say wha happening man, how life treating yer, he say not bad he still trying he luck wit de horses an dem but it look like I doing alright, so I say nar man, it might look so but I still paying rent an dat en so good, but he say well a look like a doing better dan he, so a telling im he must be backing de wrong horses, a taught I'd give him a joke an cheer him up yer no, but anyhow he en get no happier so a say I'd buy him a drink like old times, anyhow dat brighten him up a bit, so we went in a pub, wen we get inside de pub, de man start ter tell me he troubles how he was living wit some woman an how de woman take all he clothes an sell dem, an how he en have no money an no where ter live, so I say well boy yer could come an stay by me till tings ger fer de better an he fine somewhere of he own, well is den he get bright because de next ting a no is he en finish he beer, de first time a ever see him en finish a whole beer, but anyhow we go home by he an pick up he few tings an a take him round by me, but it hit me dat my girl en like him, so she en go want him sleeping wit we so wha a go do, anyhow a no de landlady had a room going spare so a wasn't worried, anyhow wen a get dey a call she aside an explain de position ter she an she say is awright if is a friend a mine, but boy some people de more yer do yer ter da help dem is de more dey let yer down, no sooner dan de man get in de house de man want ter no where all de meters is an wha kinda a locks dey have on dem, yer could beat dat, so I say well look man, yer get a room, yer get a food, well take it easy, rest yer body an see how tings go ner, but nar, he say I soft, I en have no brains, I car see further dan me eye, an I en have no business brains, so I say well if is meter yer looking ter teef from he en have no brains, because if yer teef dey go lock yer up, so better dan dey lock yer up, here look some money from me wen yer get a job pay me back, well boy if yer see de man grab de money, no sooner a take de money out me pocket, it was in he hand, so he was awright but de next ting a no is he trying ter pull de landlady in he room, one night de same one who does sing I love you baby, an I need you baby, she say she en give im no cause ter pull she in he room, but I en so sure, yer do no how people does take tings, a mean ter say he hear she singing I love you baby, I need you baby, he must be tink is he she talking bout, yer car blame de guy, so I say well look if is woman yer want why yer do ask she nice ter give yer a piece, he say he do ask no woman fer notten an he en asking no woman nice fer notten wat he want he go take an wen he want a woman he go take she, so I say look pardner it en so it go, dat if he ask he never ter no he might get it, but anyhow he en listen, so de next ting a hear is he go in de woman next ter me room an smelling up all she panties, so I see him an a say ter him look ner man, if is a woman yer want ask me an a go get one fer yer, he say he en want no woman, woman is trouble, now dat start me tinking because one minute he pulling de landlady in he room an de next he saying he en want no woman so wha he up to, so I say well look here I go give yer some money go an look fer yer own place de man start ter cry an beg me ter let him stay saying I is de only friend he ever had an how I treat him so good an how he shame he try ter take advantage a he position wit me, so I say nar man da is alright, as long as yer behave yer self an he say he go do dat so da was alright yer no wat happen, yer no wat de man do wen a tell yer some man bad dey bad yer no, de man go down stairs an tell de landlady husband how I an she carrying on but he en no I an he was mate so he come an tell me an we had a good laugh, but he en satisfy wit dat he go an tell de police how I living off prostitue an not one but two prostitue, an I living off de immoral earnings, well anyhow wen de police come ter see me, de police start ter laugh because he car see how a guy like me could have not one but two woman on de road fer him an he sorry dat he had ter trouble me so much, so I say a sorry dat he had trouble too, because wen people nice ter you, you must be nice back ter dem, so de police leave but de man en satisfy wit dat yer no wha he do, I en no where he get de letter from, he write me modder an de woman a was living wit back home an tell dem, wait fer it, he tell dem how, boy some man malicious yer no, he tell dem how I doing well an how I making a lot a money, an how I have me own house an ting, well de next ting is dey write me after all yer car blame dem dey hear dey boy making money so dey bound ter write, well anyhow dey write me an say how as a doing so well if a could send fer dem, well wha a go do a say alright, as man, a have ter send fer dem, after all, a mean ter say so anyhow a went round de corner an buy a house, an a send fer dem, so all a dem come me modder de woman a was living wit an me twelve children move in ter de house round de corner, a used ter sleep dey nights an tell dem a had work ter do at de other house, so tings start ter go good, me modder start ter do some cleaning an me woman start ter take in some washing an make some plans ter open she own launderette, so who could complain, but boy wen a tell yer dis life funny it funny yer no a get me children in a school an me woman open she launderette, so tings start ter go good, wen de next ting a hear is me friend want ter see me so I say alright, but he round de corner, yer no, an he en a three penny bus ride away, nar man de man in Brixton Prison, so a get me forms ter visit wen a get dey, de first ting de man say is how a doing, so I say yer bring me all dis way ter ask me how a doing, but he say nar man, dat en wat he want ter see me for, he say he want me ter pay a fine fer him, so I say well da is awright, how much it is, well he say is only twenty pounds, it turn out he break a meter an dey charge im twenty pounds an he couldn't pay so dey trow him inside, so I pay de fine an dey let im out, but dat en all de man want me find place fer him ter live, so I say alright, a go do dat a figure prison must a change him, put some sense in him, so a give im a room in de house me modder an dem was living in, a figure me modder could keep a eye on him during de day an I could watch im during de night, an a tell im, a say if a only catch yer near me meter, is out yer going, friend or no friend, but he say nar man, dat en go happen, he change, he en go do dat kinda ting again, how he could do a ting like dat ter me after a so nice ter him, an how if peoples nice ter yer yer must be nice ter dem, so a jump, but den a say he must be really change a mean ter say, ter hear him say a ting like dat, an a have ter believe im, after all is a ting I say meself, so a say well he really learn now, he really get de message, well boy tings start ter go good, a get me children in a school, me woman open she launderette, an de man en even going near me meters, if he want ter go ter de WC in de back just not ter pass de meter, de man going through de front door an going round, just not ter pass me meters, da is ter tell yer how good de man get, an he get nice, he get nice ter everybody, he start ter say tank you ter everybody, an smiling ter everybody, an dat en all he get a job as a nightwatchman in a factory an he even come home an say how nice de foreman is, yer could beat dat, well he beat it, he even get a job fer me modder on de factory bench, so wha a could say ter dat, a could only say well tings like, never say die, an wonders never cease, an wen mango ripe it go fall, anyhow dat en all de man even start ter pay me back me money, not in big pieces but a one here a one dere, but dat was good dat shows he was trying, he heart was in de right place, anyhow I stop tinking bout im, but a mean but yer no, one day de man pay me back a five pound note an wen a look at de five pound note well a had ter look yer no, because he never pay me back so much, wen a look at de five pound note, a see it was de same five pound note a give me wife ter put in de bank fer me, so dat hit me but a figure she must be change some money fer him, so I en worry bout it, but an a say but againg yer no, de men start ter pay me back one set a five pound notes, an all a dem is wha a give she ter put in de bank so pardner a ask yer wha a go do, wha you woulda do if all de five pound note you give yer wife ter put in de bank yer see turning up in another man hand, an is a man yer help, I help de man yer no, tell me wha you woulda do, (slight pause) yer car tink a notten, well I go tell yer wha I do or wha I was going ter do, a was going ter go over ter de pub an buy im a guiness an tell im do kill yer self, but yer no wat happen, wen a get in de pub, de man in de pub·say dey do serve black people in dis bar a have ter go round, so a hit im, an wen a hit im, he fall against a whole pile a boxes an de whole bar mash up, so da is wat a in prison for, well boy a really learn me lesson, da is de last time a go ever be nice ter anybody.

bell rings man gets up
walks off singing.   I love you baby
                          I need you baby.

Questions

1 Where is the humour in this piece? What bits of it make you laugh, and why?
2 In not more than a hundred words try to describe what happens to the narrator of this story.
3 What are the differences between the narrator and his friend? Try and describe the character of the narrator.
4 Describe some of the prejudices and racial stereotypes that are brought out in the passage.

Innocent

Anon

Will you grow up to think like me?
Will all my fears take seed and flourish
In your breast as they have in mine?
Oh my precious innocent son!
I would that attitudes have changed
So by your achievements and only so be judged
And not by the colour on show to the world.
I have struggled hard to gain respectability,
I have worked hard for life's little luxuries,
But this is now where I must carry you —
A back street slum in this fair society.
When you are grown with thoughts of your own
Please don't hold it against us,
Because we tried, we really did.
One thing was against us, just that one little thing.
No merits were placed on our law-abiding natures —
Just a minus on our unwanted colour.

Beyond the window

David McAnuff

I sometimes sit by window's ledge
When stars diffuse the sky,
And ponder my position: where I am and who am I.
For being black
I sometimes lack
The knowledge of my place.
The cause of my confusion lies within the world of race.

Beyond my sacred window
I am haunted by my fate,
Attacks of mindless violence, distant looks and local hate.
Policemen stare
With special care,
Attracted to my skin,
Ignoring any goodness that my heart may hold within.

And yet, despite my terror,
I continue on the street,
Attempt to cross the jungle, facing danger that I meet.
I play the game
And strive for fame
But can I ever be,
A fair and equal member of this light society?

So from my sheltered window
I reflect my clouded state,
Sitting in the darkness when the hours are quite late.
Where do I stand
Within this land
Will I find a pass?
Or stay with fellow victims in the world behind the glass.

Writing on the wall
Wynette Scott

Burning cars and looted shops were the magnet. They drew me home where old friends had not. Yet, I still hesitated to claim kinship with this concrete maze of my childhood. Home was the timeless dream of yielding coconut palms and flour-white beaches spoken of by my parents. Not this.

Bricks and broken bottles littered the main street like the remnants of some crazy avalanche. Television cameras greedily devoured the debris. Microphones jabbed at me. Adders after prey.

'Tell us, as a well-known member of the black community, your thoughts on the events of today.'

'What would you say is the prevailing mood of the black community at this moment in time.'

'At the end of the day, what message do you have for the volatile elements?'

Clichés. They still thought of us in terms of clichés and faceless statistics. I did what experience told me the media hated. Answered with more questions.

'Why did it take a riot to excite your interest?' and, 'What exactly do you mean by "Black Community" ?'.

They were bewildered. Sadly, I wasn't. Through the cotton wool fog of time a memory stirred. I was back to days when happiness was having no maths homework. As footsteps led me to the place in my mind, the place that I suddenly had to see, so my memories became clearer. Only half of the wall remained, in lop-sided defiance of the riot.

Each morning my mesmerized gaze had fixed on a newly discovered aspect of the wall. That particular day, it was no longer the decaying brickwork, but the jagged edges of the graffiti. Paint had dried as it dripped from each letter. All twelve of them. Three feet high and at least a mile long. Or so it seemed:

BLACKS GO HOME

Initially, the problem was passing it on the way to school. And the way home. Later, even the crises of forgotten gym kit and homework were overshadowed by the fact that it existed. What had I done to make someone go to all that trouble? I turned the corner, the wall behind me, and all but cannoned into the new black girl.

Madeleine wasn't exactly new — she'd joined us last term, but kept to herself. I faltered, not wanting to just walk on ahead. What could we talk about? For a split second I forgot the wall. She said something in that quiet voice of hers. I didn't catch it.

'How are you settling in?' I covered my confusion.

'Not too bad.' She murmured.

Oh boy. The school gates were a mirage in the distance. The silence was awkwardly long. Like the wall.

'I've forgotten my kit. Today of all days. Miss Simms'll kill me.' There was no response that I could see. I tried again.

'I'm running in the hundred and four hundred metres. Do you think she'll let me run without my shorts?'

'I hope so. You're good. Everybody says our house will win the cup.'

Well it wasn't what you'd call scintillating conversation, but it was a start. I jumped as she continued.

'Did you see the Olympics last night?'

Had I seen the Olympics? You bet I had. Common ground at last. We had both rooted for the Americans — those black athletes.

'But what about when they gave those Black Power salutes?' I was impatient for her reaction.

'What about it?' was all that she said. End of conversation. Fortunately we were at the school gates.

The bell clanged and I raced across the playground to registration. My mind was a jumbled mass of colliding thoughts as Miss Simms called the roll. Pride felt when watching the black runners conflicted with the embarrassment everyone said they had caused at the presentation. This was 1968, and 'Black is beautiful' was the chant of the day, but my mum said this was carrying it too far. The emotion aroused by the wall returned. An elbow dug into my ribs. 'Yes Miss'. Out of the daydream, I automatically responded to my name.

Closing the register, Miss Simms told us that the timetable had been rearranged. We could practice for the interhouse sports until lunchtime.

'Any questions?' her eyes fired a challenge. I took a deep breath.

'Please Miss, I've forgotten my things.'

'Things? You don't mean your gym kit?' I nodded guiltily.

'I should have guessed. Has anyone got a spare pair of shorts to lend to this stupid child?' she appealed to the class, then almost interrupted herself.

'On second thoughts, you don't deserve to represent your house if this is any indication of your enthusiasm.' It got worse. 'I've had nothing but complaints over the last few days about your attitude. Take my advice. Pull your socks up my girl, or there'll be trouble. Is that clear?'

It was. Maybe Miss Simms had painted the wall, the old battle-axe. I couldn't define it, but there was always a different tone in her voice when she spoke to us blacks.

'And take that smirk off your face this instant!' I did my best, but not being sure what a 'smirk' was, my success was doubtful.

In regimented lines, we marched to assembly across the playground triangle. The sight of all the classes together always reminded me of a zebra's stripes — the classes with even numbers had mostly black kids, while the odd numbered classes which were the A streams, had mostly whites. I once heard Miss Simms say that this 'phenomenon' was a remarkable coincidence, but I never understood what she meant.

I sat vaguely miserable in the changing room, watching the others get ready. There was Madeleine. The handful of black girls in the class tended to stick together, but not her. Paulette, Joy and Merline giggled, and from time to time she would rocket a glance in their direction. They never looked at her. Miss Simms came in.

'Chop chop! We're going to hold trials to see who can take Rosalyn's place in the sports. Out with you!'

Only four girls were any good, and Madeleine was easily the best of those. Watching her streak to the tape, I asked Paulette what she thought of the new girl.

'Man she can run.' Paulette clapped and jumped up and down. 'Maybe she'll get us some good points.'

Not having to change, I was first in the dining-hall. As usual, I kept three places for my friends. For some reason Madeleine came to mind, and I placed a book on another chair. I was taken aback to see the subject of my thoughts enter surrounded by Paulette and the others. They were talking excitedly about our chances in the games. She didn't say very much.

We did win the cup. Madeleine's contribution proved crucial to the final outcome. My disappointment at not taking part was forgotten as I cheered her home, my lungs bursting for lack of air.

At home-time I waited for her at the gates. She saw me but went to walk past.

'Hey, hang on!'

'How come suddenly everyone wants to be my friend?' The voice was no longer quiet. At first I was stuck for a reply, then I worked it out aloud.

'Because of the games, I suppose. But I was pleased for you, not the house. No one can take today away from you.' I felt a rising pain as the child that I had been started to leave me.

Her jaw unclenched. She talked then about many things. About the other black kids rejecting her because she came from a different island to them; how they made fun of her accent.

'That's why I talk quiet.' She finished. 'Until today.' I had to convince her that I knew how she felt.

'My family is from the same place that they come from, but I was born here. Sometimes I can't join in when they talk about "back home".'

We looked at each other. In many ways, life was not just black or white. There were all the in between shades.

'Anyway' Madeleine said, 'I'm not going to change what I feel about my country just because I'm not there anymore.'

We parted at the crossroads. Funny, for the first time in ages, I couldn't remember passing the wall. I did remember the Olympic athletes showing in the only way they knew how pride in a country left three hundred years before. The last vestige of childhood vanished into the early evening sunset.

The house cup was the talking point of assembly the next day. Afterwards, Merline said to me, 'When we collected our medals, it was just like on telly. What about those black athletes giving those Black Power salutes in front of that massive crowd?'

'What about it?' I shrugged.

Just one more single memory detached itself from those days that seemed to be a century before. My careers teacher — a vision of lacquered perfection — asked me what I would do when I left school.

'Something to help, make things better.' There was no hesitation.

Momentary dissatisfaction creased her pan-stick make-up. 'You mean, you want to be a nurse?'

I nodded. Anything to escape. Like the media, like Miss Simms and even like Merline, she hadn't noticed the writing on the wall. I had.

I turned, walking away from it without a backward glance.

Questions

1 In no more than 150 words, try to explain why the writer chose her title for this story.

2 What can you learn from reading this story?

My enemy

Mustapha Matura

Characters
A (Sir William Hardback)
B
C
MB (Mustafa Black)

Scene one

A   (The office of a television producer)
A   Have you the reports from the Legal Dept?
B   Yes here they are.
A   Are they quite sure about this?
B   Yes quite sure, they've had their best boys on it. I think they rather enjoyed it; the challenge you know.
A   Yes I know. How much time till transmission?
B   One hour.
A   Right. I think we have him, this is very good, very good. Is he here yet?
B   Yes he's been given the usual softening treatment, drinks and so on, you know.
A   Yes, I know.
B   Funny though, he's refused the drink, Do you think he knows?
A   I don't know, I don't want to know. I have got him where I want him, he has to answer my questions honestly or lose respect with his people and that's just where I want him, honest as hell.
B   Is he still seeing her?
A   He's not seeing her, she's seeing him. I've tried the father role, the friend role, I've even had her uncle come down from the country.
B   No go.
A   No go. It's like she's blind.
B   Have you tried sending her away, to Switzerland maybe?
A   My dear fellow, the days when one sends one's daughter to Switzerland because she can't leave a black alone are over. Besides, they all have embassies all over the place now.

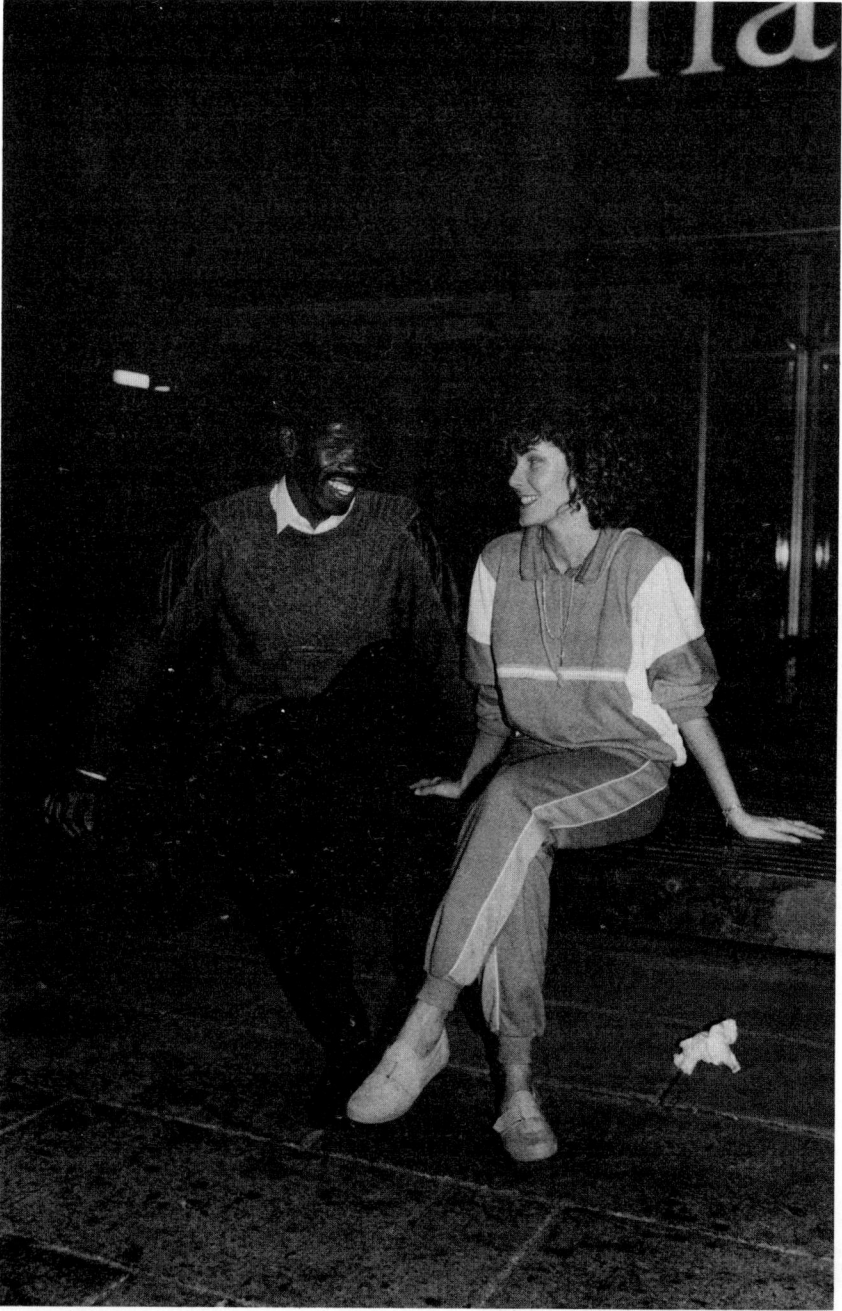

B	Yes, what about drugs?
A	What about drugs?
B	Well, have you tried getting him on that? It's known.
A	It's also known my daughter is seeing him. If it comes out that he takes drugs, people will think she takes them too. No, this is just perfect, in front of a cool million people.
	(Knock, then shout, 'Fifteen minutes, Sir').
A	Come on let's go.
B	Have you got everything, Sir?
A	Yes.
	(Fade)
C	Good evening ladies and gentlemen. Tonight, PEOPLE presents another face to face interview with someone in the news. Tonight it is the self-styled Prime Minister of the Black Nation of Britain, Mustafa Black, and asking the questions tonight will be that well known Member of Parliament Sir William Hardback, QC, MP
	(Applause)
A	Good evening, Mr Black.
MB	Not Mister, just Black, or Mustafa will do.
A	Well Mustafa, I take it that is not your real name.
MB	It is not the name I was given at birth, but it is my real name.
A	Why did you change your name given at birth and why have you chosen the one you now use?
MB	Because you must know by now that the plantation owners and slave owners gave their names to their slaves and I don't choose to carry the name of my enemy. Mustafa because I am a Muslim, and Black because I am black.
A	But if every black man took the name Black, there will be all sorts of confusion.
	(Laughter)
MB	Is that a question?
A	No. Just thinking aloud.
A	As you know, we already have a Prime Minister in this country. What makes you think we need another?
MB	Your Prime Minister does not represent us, the Black Nation of Britain. He represents our enemies, so my people thought about it and we elected a council which I am proud to serve.
A	What are your policies?
MB	My council has many policies, but the basic overall underlying principle is freedom for all black people in this country and all

over the world, freedom and respect, and all our policies are aimed towards achieving that goal.

A   Would you serve the white people of this nation?

MB   They already have a Prime Minister.

A   Are you a better Prime Minister?

MB   I would like to make the record straight at this moment. I am not a Prime Minister. I am merely a chief, and we have a council not a government, that is another fabrication by the enemy press that needs clearing up.

A   It's been said that you train your followers to fight. Is that true?

MB   We train our warriors to defend themselves. We have found it necessary to do so. The enemy police neither protect nor defend us so we have to do it ourselves. By and large we have found this the best way, best for us and best for our enemies.

A   In what way is it best?

MB   Well, when we defend ourselves we seem to make a better job of it and best for our enemies because we do it so well they don't attack us so often.

A   Have you arms?

MB   No we have no arms, we are not rich enough to purchase arms, and even if we were I don't think the arms dealers of the world who are in fact our enemies would sell us any, so we have no arms.

A   Have you been offered arms by any outside government? Your deputy has just come back from a visit to China. Did the Chinese government offer you arms?

MB   My brother went to China to have talks with the leaders there and to see how the revolution is taking shape. He is off to Cuba and Algiers next.

A   Do you foresee any situation whereby your community and the white people could live in peace without tension?

MB   Yes when the people of this country and all over this world accept the fact that we are people, human beings, and treat us as such with respect and honesty then you will have a real and peaceful society. That's all that's needed, respect and trust.

A   Do you foresee any situation whereby your community and the white people would be in open conflict?

MB   You mean a physical scene — arms and all that. Yes I do if our enemies continue their policies of wilful disregard for our feelings and wishes and continue their policy of lies, half lies and full lies. I see no other course than an open conflict. It is a basic issue of reality versus fantasy, our enemies openly preach human kindness and understanding and openly do and enact things that create unhappiness and death and suffering. So what are we to believe — what they say or what happens as a result of their acts and thoughts? What is real — what they say, and it's only our imagination that black people are suffering, starving, being shot and tortured and humiliated by the same people that preach love and understanding? That is what we face today, this deceit, this beautiful thought and horrible action, this great tolerance and this revolting humiliation, this nice world and the open acts of oppression and submission, that is what we face. We know which is real, we know how hard the stick is not the person who uses it, it's the person who receives it.

A   Then I take it that you do not rule out armed retaliation.

MB   I rule out nothing. Our enemies have seen fit to use arms against us to further and secure their position. I see no reason why we should continue playing the goodie, when in fact we have been playing the baddie.

A   I don't follow you. How have you been playing the baddie?

MB   By being what we were supposed to be, and not what we were. We allowed ourselves to be manoeuvred into a position where we appeared bad when we were being ourselves and that cannot be suppressed easily and that was made to seem bad by our enemies so when we did what was thought good we in fact were fooling our enemies, but as it turned out at our own expense, if you know what I mean.

A   I don't quite follow you but we'll pass on to something else. How do you see your people developing in the next ten years?

MB   I want to see the complete absence of a black middle class. They have been the chains on us, they have always held themselves back and by presenting this unreal front of false respectability lulled the poor blacks to aspire to their position and thereby creating a never ending circle of nothingness. I want to see a society structured on the lines of a wise many and a willing to learn few, as it is now we have the wise few and the unwilling to learn many but the reality of the situation has never once denied their suspicion, when we suspect dishonesty when something looks fishy and we lift the stone we see a snake. We have never once lifted a stone and seen a dove. Snakes all the time. So now what we do is just leave the stone alone and watch it. After a while it crawls out on its own accord, fear for one thing brings it out, fear we might smash that same stone. It's very amusing to observe, but we have no more time for these games, they are negative and destructive. What we have to do now is to start facing the situation as it is, not how we would like it to be or how we think it is but how it is and that is something we have never done before, but now is the time, the time is now.

A   I would just like to end on one final question. Would you tell your people, the black people of this country, the people you represent, to take arms against the white people of this country, and I would like a clear answer.

MB   Yes, I would tell my people to take arms. I would even take arms myself against all our enemies.

A   Who are your enemies?

MB   All oppressors and murderers of black people all over the world are my enemies.

A   I did ask for a clear answer, but I suppose I'll have to accept that one. Well that brings us to the end of PEOPLE for tonight. Join us for another evening of interesting viewing next week same time. Good night. Da da DAA da Daa DaaaaDa da daaa.

Questions

1 What is this sketch attempting to show?
2 Who is the 'enemy' of the title. What is he trying to do, and how successful is he?
3 Do you disagree with or object to any of the sentiments expressed in the sketch? Give reasons for your opinions.